CALM IN CHAOS

Daily Practices for Mindfulness and Mental Well-being

S Nikolson

Kindle

INTRODUCTION

In today's fast-paced and chaotic world, many of us are caught in a whirlwind of endless to-do lists, overwhelming responsibilities, and constant distractions. We are bombarded by information from every direction, our minds cluttered with worries about the future and regrets from the past. Finding calm and balance can feel impossible during this chaos, but it does not have to be.

This book, *Calm in Chaos: Daily Practices for Mindfulness and Mental Well-being*, is designed to help you do just that—find calm, clarity, and resilience in the face of life's challenges. Mindfulness is the key. It is a practice that invites you to slow down, breathe deeply, and become fully present in the moment, no matter what is happening around you. Through consistent mindfulness practice, you can better train your mind to navigate stress, anxiety, and emotional turbulence, ultimately fostering a sense of inner peace.

Mindfulness has been practiced for thousands of years, rooted in ancient meditation traditions, yet it has become increasingly relevant in our modern world. Research has shown that mindfulness profoundly affects mental and physical health in recent decades. Studies reveal that mindfulness reduces stress, enhances emotional resilience, improves focus, and promotes well-being. However, beyond science, mindfulness offers a simple, practical solution to many of the challenges we face today: It teaches us to live in the present moment.

When you practice mindfulness, you train your brain to break free from automatic thought patterns that often drive feelings of stress, anxiety, and dissatisfaction. Instead of reacting to every challenge or stressor with tension, you learn to respond calmly and clearly. The more you practice, the more you build the capacity to stay grounded, centered, and peaceful—even in the most chaotic circumstances.

Calm in Chaos is not just another self-help book. It is a toolkit designed to offer practical, daily mindfulness practices you can integrate into your life. Whether juggling a demanding job, parenting, or simply navigating the stressors of daily living, the exercises in this book are meant to be simple, accessible, and applicable to your everyday routine.

Each chapter will introduce you to mindfulness techniques such as meditation, mindful breathing, body scans, and mindful movement. However, more importantly, it will show you how to weave these practices into your day, transforming the most ordinary moments—like eating, walking, or even washing the dishes—into opportunities for mindfulness and mental well-being.

As you move through the book, you will learn how to:
- Cultivate mindfulness to reduce stress and anxiety
- Develop emotional resilience in the face of challenges
- Stay present and focused amidst distractions
- Manage difficult emotions with greater compassion and awareness
- Build mental clarity, creativity, and balance

The goal of this book is not to overwhelm you with techniques but to offer a pathway to sustainable, meaningful change. Mindfulness is not a one-size-fits-all solution. This practice can be personalized to fit your unique lifestyle and needs. As you read, you will discover that you do not need to set aside hours daily to meditate or attend a silent retreat to see the benefits. Even a few minutes of mindfulness practice can create significant shifts in how you feel and relate to your thoughts and emotions.

The key is consistency. Mindfulness, like any skill, grows stronger with regular practice. As you commit to these daily practices, you will notice small and powerful changes—perhaps you will find yourself less reactive when faced with a stressful situation, or you will experience moments of peace amidst the busyness of your day. Over time, these small shifts can lead to profound, lasting transformations in your mental and emotional well-being.

At its core, *Calm in Chaos* invites you to slow down, breathe, connect with yourself, and embrace the present moment, no matter what it holds. This book reminds us that no matter how busy or chaotic life becomes, there is always the possibility of finding peace. You do not have to wait for the perfect conditions to feel calm—you can create calmness within yourself right now.

As you begin this journey into mindfulness, remember that it is not about perfection. You will have days when your mind feels too scattered to focus on, or life's challenges seem too big to handle. That is okay. Mindfulness is about being with whatever arises, without judgment or expectation. It is about learning to accept yourself, your thoughts, and your emotions with compassion, even in moments of difficulty.

So, take a deep breath, settle into the present moment, and open your mind to the possibilities of mindfulness. The journey to greater calm, clarity, and well-being begins now.

Welcome to *Calm in Chaos*. Let us begin.

CHAPTER 1:
MINDFULNESS IN THE MODERN WORLD:
A POWERFUL TOOL FOR WELL-BEING

In today's fast-paced, hyper-connected world, mindfulness has emerged as an antidote to the pressures of modern life. As demands on attention and productivity grow, individuals are increasingly overwhelmed by constant connectivity, rapid technological advancements, and an ever-growing information stream. This has resulted in heightened levels of stress, anxiety, and an inability to remain present in daily life (Markowetz et al., 2014). Mindfulness has gained significant popularity in this environment, offering a much-needed counterbalance. Centered on paying attention to the present moment with non-judgmental awareness, mindfulness provides individuals the tools to cultivate calm, reduce stress, and foster emotional and physical well-being (Kabat-Zinn, 2003).

The Attention Economy and Digital Distractions

The modern era has seen the rise of what some researchers call the "attention economy," where smartphones, social media, and the internet demand constant engagement (Markowetz et al., 2014). The average person checks their phone hundreds of times daily, often without any need. This continuous digital engagement fragments attention, exacerbates stress, and contributes to feelings of anxiety, making it increasingly difficult to focus on the present moment (Levy et al., 2012). Research shows constant interruptions can reduce productivity and affect well-being (Rosen et al., 2008).

Mindfulness offers a way to regain control of one's attention by encouraging individuals to become more conscious of how they spend their mental energy. It teaches people to step back, notice their thoughts, and redirect their attention intentionally, which helps reduce mindless engagement with digital devices (Gelles, 2015). This deliberate disengagement from distractions allows individuals to focus on meaningful activities and reduces stress. A study by Levy et al. (2012) found that participants who underwent mindfulness training reported improved attention and a more remarkable ability to manage digital distractions, leading to enhanced focus and productivity.

Mindfulness in the Workplace

The workplace has become critical where mindfulness is applied to address stress and improve employee well-being. Long hours, demanding deadlines, and constant connectivity have led to widespread industry burnout (Good et al., 2016). Many companies, including Google, Aetna, and Intel, have recognized the potential of mindfulness programs to reduce stress and enhance productivity. These programs often include mindfulness meditation, mindful communication workshops, and techniques for managing workplace stress (Gelles, 2015).

Studies show that mindfulness in the workplace leads to significant improvements in employee well-being. For example, Aetna's mindfulness program resulted in a 28% reduction in stress levels among participants, a 20% improvement in sleep quality, and a 62-minute increase in weekly productivity (Gelles, 2015). Research supports these findings, showing that workplace mindfulness programs can reduce employee burnout and improve job satisfaction (Good et al., 2016).

Mindfulness also fosters emotional intelligence and resilience in the workplace, which are critical for effective leadership and team collaboration. Leaders who practice mindfulness develop greater self-awareness, empathy, and an enhanced ability to remain calm under pressure (Boyatzis & McKee, 2005). Reb et al. (2014) found that mindfulness helps leaders improve decision-making by enhancing their capacity to process information and make thoughtful decisions under stress. This calm, deliberate decision-making improves leadership effectiveness, promotes a positive work culture, and enhances team dynamics.

In addition, employees who practice mindfulness are better communicators and more collaborative. Mindfulness encourages non-reactive listening and emotional regulation, improving colleagues' relationships and fostering a supportive, inclusive work environment (Good et al., 2016). Organizations that incorporate mindfulness often report lower turnover rates, higher employee engagement, and a more positive organizational atmosphere (Kegan et al., 2014).

Mindfulness in Education

The benefits of mindfulness extend to education, where students face various challenges, including academic pressure, social stress, and digital distractions. Mindfulness programs in schools have gained popularity as tools for improving focus, emotional regulation, and overall well-being among students (Zenner et al., 2014). Mindfulness techniques such as mindful breathing, body scans, and mindful listening help students manage stress, reduce anxiety, and improve academic performance (Zenner et al., 2014).

A key benefit of mindfulness in education is its ability to enhance students' self-awareness and emotional intelligence. By teaching students to observe their thoughts and emotions without judgment, mindfulness fosters emotional regulation and resilience, essential skills for navigating the challenges of adolescence (Roeser et al., 2012). Research has shown that mindfulness students demonstrate improved attention, reduced anxiety, and enhanced emotional well-being, positively impacting their academic performance (Zenner et al., 2014).

Mindfulness also benefits educators by helping them manage classroom dynamics more effectively. Mindfulness teachers report greater empathy for their students, improved emotional resilience, and a more vital ability to create a supportive, nurturing classroom environment (Roeser et al., 2012). These improvements lead to better student-teacher relationships and a more positive learning atmosphere, fostering students' academic and emotional growth.

Mindfulness in Healthcare

The healthcare sector has increasingly adopted mindfulness to manage chronic conditions, reduce stress, and improve patient outcomes. Mindfulness-based interventions (MBIs), such as Mindfulness-Based Stress Reduction (MBSR) and Mindfulness-Based Cognitive Therapy (MBCT), have been widely implemented in clinical settings to help patients cope with mental health conditions like anxiety and depression, as well as chronic pain (Kabat-Zinn, 1990; Teasdale et al., 2000). These interventions teach patients to observe their thoughts and emotions without judgment, helping them interrupt negative thought patterns and reduce stress (Hofmann et al., 2010).

One of the most well-documented uses of mindfulness is in treating mental health disorders, including anxiety, depression, and post-traumatic stress disorder (PTSD). Mindfulness-Based Cognitive Therapy (MBCT) is as effective as antidepressant medication in preventing depression relapse (Kuyken et al., 2015). For individuals with PTSD, mindfulness helps reduce hyperarousal and emotional reactivity, providing a non-reactive space to process traumatic memories (King et al., 2013).

Mindfulness has also proven highly beneficial in managing chronic pain. Pain is a multifaceted experience influenced by both physical and emotional factors. Mindfulness helps patients change their relationship with pain by encouraging them to observe it without resistance or attachment (Kabat-Zinn, 1990). This shift in perspective can significantly reduce the emotional distress associated with chronic pain, leading to improved quality of life. Research shows that mindfulness-based interventions reduce pain intensity and pain-related distress for individuals with conditions such as fibromyalgia, arthritis, and lower back pain (Cherkin et al., 2016).

Beyond mental health and pain management, mindfulness supports physical health by reducing blood pressure, improving immune function, and enhancing overall well-being. High blood pressure, a significant risk factor for cardiovascular disease, can be effectively reduced through mindfulness practices, which promote relaxation and stress reduction (Hughes et al., 2010). Furthermore, studies show that mindfulness enhances immune system function, making individuals more resilient to infections and illnesses (Davidson et al., 2003).

Mindfulness also improves sleep quality, essential for mental and physical health. Chronic sleep deprivation is linked to various health problems, including obesity, diabetes, and cognitive decline. Mindfulness helps individuals cultivate a sense of relaxation, making falling and staying asleep easier. Research indicates that mindfulness-based interventions are highly effective in treating insomnia and improving overall sleep quality (Ong et al., 2014).

The Role of Mindfulness in Preventive Healthcare

As healthcare shifts from treatment to prevention, mindfulness is increasingly recognized as a valuable tool for preventive medicine. Lifestyle factors, including poor diet, lack of exercise, and chronic stress, often drive chronic diseases such as diabetes, cardiovascular disease, and obesity. Mindfulness addresses these underlying causes by promoting healthier behaviors and reducing the negative impact of stress on the body (Kristeller & Wolever, 2010).

Mindful eating is one example of how mindfulness can

encourage healthier habits. By paying close attention to eating, individuals become more aware of hunger and satiety cues, leading to more nutritious food choices and reduced emotional eating (Kristeller & Wolever, 2010). Similarly, mindfulness enhances motivation for physical activity by increasing body awareness, making exercise more enjoyable and engaging.

Reflection and Personal Practice

Mindfulness is a versatile and accessible practice that can be integrated into daily life in many ways. Whether through structured meditation, mindful walking, or taking a few moments for deep breathing, mindfulness offers countless opportunities for cultivating presence and self-awareness. For beginners, starting with a simple breathing exercise can help develop mindfulness practice (Kabat-Zinn, 1990). Over time, more advanced techniques such as body scans or loving-kindness meditation can deepen the practice and bring additional benefits (Teasdale et al., 2000).

Mindful eating is another practice that can easily be incorporated into daily routines. Taking time to savor each bite and paying attention to the textures and flavors of food allows individuals to develop a healthier relationship with eating. This practice improves dietary habits and fosters greater body awareness and appreciation (Kristeller & Wolever, 2010).

It is important to remember that mindfulness is a practice, not a goal. The key is maintaining a non-judgmental awareness of thoughts, feelings, and sensations, even when the mind feels scattered or distracted. Regular mindfulness builds emotional resilience, reduces stress, and improves overall well-being.

References:

- Baer, R. A. (2003). Mindfulness training as a clinical intervention: A conceptual and empirical review. *Clinical Psychology: Science and Practice*, 10(2), 125–143.

- Bodhi, B. (2010). *The Noble Eightfold Path: Way to the End of Suffering*. Pariyatti Publishing.

- Cherkin, D. C., Sherman, K. J., Balderson, B. H., Cook, A. J., Anderson, M. L., Hawkes, R. J., & Turner, J. A. (2016). Effect of mindfulness-based stress reduction vs cognitive behavioral therapy or usual care on back pain and functional limitations in adults with chronic low back pain. *JAMA*, 315(12), 1240-1249.

- Creswell, J. D. (2017). Mindfulness interventions. *Annual Review of Psychology*, 68, 491-516.

- Davidson, R. J., Kabat-Zinn, J., Schumacher, J., Rosenkranz, M., Muller, D., Santorelli, S. F., & Sheridan, J. F. (2003). Alterations in brain and immune function produced by mindfulness meditation. *Psychosomatic Medicine*, 65(4), 564-570.

- Gelles, D. (2015). *Mindful Work: How Meditation is Changing Business from the Inside Out*. Houghton Mifflin Harcourt.

- Good, D. J., Lyddy, C. J., Glomb, T. M., Bono, J. E., Brown, K. W., Duffy, M. K., & Lazar, S. W. (2016). Contemplating mindfulness at work: An integrative review. *Journal of Management*, 42(1), 114-142.

- Hofmann, S. G., Sawyer, A. T., Witt, A. A., & Oh, D. (2010). The effect of mindfulness-based therapy on anxiety and depression: A meta-analytic review. *Journal of Consulting and Clinical Psychology*, 78(2), 169.

- Kabat-Zinn, J. (1990). *Whole Catastrophe Living: Using the Wisdom of Your Body and Mind to Face Stress, Pain, and Illness*. Delacorte Press.

- King, A. P., Erickson, T. M., Giardino, N. D., Favorite, T., Rauch, S. A., Robinson, E., & Liberzon, I. (2013). A pilot study of group mindfulness-based cognitive therapy (MBCT) for combat veterans with posttraumatic stress disorder (PTSD). *Depression and Anxiety*, 30(7), 638-645.

- Kristeller, J. L., & Wolever, R. Q. (2010). Mindfulness-based eating awareness training for treating binge eating disorder: The conceptual foundation. *Eating Disorders*, 19(1), 49-61.

- Levy, D. M., & Wobbrock, J. O. (2012). Mindfulness in the workplace. *Proceedings of the ACM*, 5(1), 1–10.

- Markowetz, A., Błaszkiewicz, K., Montag, C., Switala, C., & Schlaepfer, T. E. (2014). Psycho-informatics: Big data shaping modern psychometrics. *Medical Hypotheses*, 82(4), 405-411.

- Ong, J. C., Shapiro, S. L., & Manber, R. (2014). Combining mindfulness meditation with cognitive-behavior therapy for insomnia: A treatment-development study. *Behavior Therapy*, 39(2), 171–182.

- Reb, J., Narayanan, J., & Chaturvedi, S. (2014). Leading mindfully: Two studies on the influence of supervisor trait mindfulness on employee well-being and performance. *Mindfulness*, 5(1), 36–45.

- Roeser, R. W., Skinner, E., Beers, J., & Jennings, P. A. (2012). Mindfulness training and teachers' professional development: An emerging area of research and practice. *Child Development Perspectives*, 6(2), 167-173.

- Zenner, C., Herrnleben-Kurz, S., & Walach, H. (2014). Mindfulness-based interventions in schools—a systematic review and meta-analysis. *Frontiers in Psychology*, 5, 603.

CHAPTER 2: UNDERSTANDING THE MIND-BODY CONNECTION

Introduction to the Mind-Body Connection

The intricate relationship between the mind and body has been a subject of fascination for centuries, transcending cultures, medical disciplines, and philosophical schools of thought. Historically, the mind-body connection was primarily the domain of ancient Eastern philosophies like Taoism, Buddhism, and Ayurveda, where it was understood that one's mental and emotional states are deeply intertwined with physical health. In recent years, this concept has gained traction in Western science and medicine as a growing body of research highlights the inextricable link between our mental well-being and physical condition. Understanding and nurturing this connection offers profound insights into achieving holistic health and well-being.

At the heart of the mind-body connection is the idea that the brain and body constantly communicate, and this dialogue plays a crucial role in how we experience and respond to the world. For instance, when we face stressful situations, our brains perceive these challenges and trigger physical responses such as muscle tension, increased heart rate, and changes in hormone levels. Likewise, when our bodies experience pain or discomfort, it can profoundly influence our emotional state, leading to feelings of frustration, sadness, or anxiety.

Eastern practices like yoga, qi gong, and tai chi have long emphasized the unity of mind and body, teaching individuals to cultivate awareness of their physical and mental states through mindful movement and breathwork. These practices harmonize the body's energy, promoting balance, relaxation, and resilience. In yoga, for example, the asanas (physical postures) serve as a vehicle for inner exploration, allowing practitioners to observe how their bodies react to different movements and postures while also quieting the mind. Yoga's meditative nature encourages an integrated approach to health, where emotional and mental well-being are critical components of physical health.

Similarly, qi gong, an ancient Chinese practice that combines slow, deliberate movements with deep breathing, cultivates the body's qi (life force energy). Qi gong practitioners believe that maintaining a steady flow of energy throughout the body can prevent illness, relieve pain, and restore physical and mental balance. This philosophy is rooted in traditional Chinese medicine, which posits that blockages in the energy flow can lead to physical and emotional ailments.

In modern times, scientific advances have confirmed much of what these ancient practices intuitively understood. Psychoneuroimmunology (PNI), a burgeoning field of study, explores how psychological factors like stress, anxiety, and depression can influence immune function and overall physical health. PNI research shows that chronic stress, for example, can weaken the immune system, making individuals more susceptible to infections and illnesses. Conversely, positive mental states such as optimism and emotional resilience have been associated with better health outcomes, including faster recovery from illness and lower incidences of chronic disease (Creswell et al., 2012).

One of the most compelling aspects of the mind-body connection is how it influences healing. Studies have shown that individuals with a strong belief in their ability to recover from illness often fare better than those who feel helpless or pessimistic. This phenomenon, known as the placebo effect, demonstrates the power of the mind in shaping physical outcomes. When patients believe that a treatment will help them, their brains can release chemicals that mimic the effects of the treatment itself, leading to real improvements in their condition. This underscores the importance of mental and emotional states in the healing process.

Furthermore, the mind-body connection offers a valuable framework for understanding and treating chronic conditions such as chronic pain, fibromyalgia, and irritable bowel syndrome (IBS), where physical symptoms are often closely tied to emotional stressors. By addressing both the physical and emotional dimensions of these conditions, healthcare providers can offer more holistic and effective treatments. For example, mindfulness-based interventions such as Mindfulness-Based Stress Reduction (MBSR) have been shown to reduce pain intensity, improve emotional resilience, and enhance overall quality of life for individuals suffering from chronic pain (Kabat-Zinn, 1985).

As we delve deeper into the mind-body connection, it becomes clear that fostering this relationship is a philosophical exercise and a practical tool for achieving excellent health and well-being. Tuning into the mind and body offers profound benefits that can improve our mental and physical health, whether through mindfulness, yoga, or meditation.

How Stress Manifests Physically

Stress is an inevitable part of life. Stress can significantly affect the mind and body, whether caused by work pressures, family responsibilities, or health challenges. While many people think of stress as a purely emotional or mental experience, its effects are often felt acutely in the body. Chronic stress can manifest in a variety of physical symptoms that, over time, may lead to serious health problems.

The body's stress response, often called the fight-or-flight response, is a natural physiological reaction to perceived threats. When we encounter a stressful situation, our brain sends signals to the adrenal glands to release stress hormones such as cortisol and adrenaline. These hormones prepare the body to confront the threat (fight) or flee from it (flight) by increasing heart rate, blood pressure, and energy supplies. While this response is crucial for survival in short-term situations, it can be harmful if activated repeatedly or over long periods, as is often the case in modern life.

One of the most common ways stress manifests physically is through muscle tension. Many individuals unknowingly carry tension in their neck, shoulders, and back because of stress. This persistent tightness can lead to discomfort, stiffness, and even chronic pain. Stress-related muscle tension is often accompanied by headaches or migraines, which are frequently triggered by prolonged periods of physical and emotional strain. Over time, this tension can contribute to long-term conditions such as temporomandibular joint dysfunction (TMJ) or fibromyalgia, which are often exacerbated by stress (Kroenke et al., 2003).

Stress also takes a toll on the cardiovascular system. When the body is tense, blood pressure rises, and the heart works harder to pump blood. While this is beneficial in a life-threatening situation, chronic stress can contribute to long-term heart problems, including hypertension, heart disease, and stroke. Research has shown that individuals with high levels of chronic stress are at greater risk of developing heart conditions, with stress-related behaviors such as smoking, overeating, and lack of exercise further compounding the problem (Steptoe & Kivimäki, 2012).

Another area where stress manifests physically is in the digestive system. The gut is often called the "second brain" because of its close relationship with the central nervous system. When we are stressed, the digestive system can become dysregulated, leading to symptoms like indigestion, heartburn, nausea, and irritable bowel syndrome (IBS). Stress is one of the leading causes of IBS, a condition characterized by chronic abdominal pain, bloating, and irregular bowel movements. The gut-brain connection highlights how closely the mind and digestive system are linked, with stress often aggravating or triggering digestive issues (Mayer et al., 2001).

Moreover, chronic stress weakens the immune system, making the body more vulnerable to infections and illnesses. Stress hormones like cortisol suppress immune function by reducing the production of cytokines, proteins that regulate immune responses. This can leave individuals more susceptible to colds, infections, and other illnesses. Studies have shown that individuals with high levels of stress tend to take longer to recover from diseases and are more prone to complications (Cohen et al., 2012). Additionally, chronic stress has been linked to the progression of autoimmune diseases such as rheumatoid arthritis and lupus, where the immune system mistakenly attacks the body's tissues.

The long-term effects of stress on physical health cannot be overstated. Over time, chronic stress can contribute to the development of severe health conditions, including diabetes, obesity, depression, and even cancer. While essential for short-term survival, the stress response is not meant to be activated continuously. When it is, the body's resources become depleted, leading to many physical ailments.

Understanding how stress manifests physically is the first step toward managing it effectively. By recognizing the signs of stress in the body—whether it is tension in the shoulders, digestive issues, or frequent headaches—individuals can take proactive steps to reduce stress and prevent long-term health consequences.

Mindfulness Practices for Physical Awareness

One of the most effective ways to address the physical effects of stress is through mindfulness practices that cultivate physical awareness. Mindfulness involves paying attention to the present moment and acknowledging thoughts, feelings, and bodily sensations without judgment. By practicing mindfulness, individuals can develop a deeper connection with their bodies, learning to recognize the early signs of stress and tension before they escalate into more severe health issues.

There are several mindfulness practices specifically designed to enhance physical awareness. One of the most widely used techniques is the body scan, a mindfulness exercise focusing attention on different body parts. The body scan allows individuals to systematically observe sensations in the body, such as tension, warmth, or discomfort, without trying to change or fix them. Instead, the goal is to notice these sensations and cultivate a non-judgmental awareness.

To practice a body scan, find a quiet space to sit or lie comfortably. Close your eyes and take a few deep breaths to center yourself. Begin by focusing on the sensation of your breath as it moves in and out of your body. Then, starting at the top of your head, slowly bring your attention to different body parts, moving through your neck, shoulders, arms, chest, abdomen, legs, and feet. As you focus on each area, notice any sensations you may feel—tension, tingling, warmth, or coolness. If you encounter areas of discomfort, acknowledge them without judgment or the need to "fix" them. After scanning the entire body, take a few moments to notice how you feel before gently opening your eyes.

The body scan is an excellent tool for identifying areas of tension or stress in the body. By regularly practicing this exercise, individuals can become more attuned to their physical state and take steps to alleviate tension before it leads to more severe issues.

Another mindfulness practice that promotes physical awareness is progressive muscle relaxation (PMR). This technique involves tensing and then relaxing different muscle groups in the body, which can help to reduce physical tension and stress. By intentionally tightening and releasing muscles, PMR enables individuals to become more aware of where they hold tension and how to release it. The practice also encourages deep relaxation, alleviating physical and mental stress.

Start by finding a quiet, comfortable space to practice progressive muscle relaxation. Take a few deep breaths to center yourself. Begin by focusing on your feet. Tense the muscles in your feet by curling your toes and holding the tension for about five seconds. Then, release the tension and notice the sensation of relaxation in your feet. Continue this process, moving your body through your calves, thighs, abdomen, chest, arms, and face. Each time, tense the muscles for a few seconds, then release and focus on the feeling of relaxation. By the end of the exercise, your entire body should feel more relaxed and at ease.

PMR is particularly beneficial for those who experience chronic muscle tension or stress-related pain. By consciously releasing muscle tension, individuals can reduce physical discomfort and promote a sense of calm and relaxation. This technique is often combined with other mindfulness practices, such as body scans or breathing exercises, to enhance overall well-being.

In addition to the body scan and PMR, mindful stretching is another effective way to enhance physical awareness and relieve stress. Mindful stretching involves performing simple stretches while paying close attention to the sensations in the body. The goal is to stretch in a comfortable and nurturing way without forcing the body into uncomfortable positions. By focusing on the breath and stretching sensations, individuals can release tension and cultivate a greater sense of presence in the body.

To practice mindful stretching, choose simple stretches, such as reaching your arms overhead, bending forward, or stretching your legs. As you stretch, focus on the sensation of the muscles lengthening and releasing. Pay attention to how your body feels in each stretch, noticing areas of tightness or discomfort without judgment. Breathe deeply and slowly as you stretch, allowing the breath to guide your movements. Mindful stretching is not about achieving a perfect pose but exploring how your body feels in the present moment.

These mindfulness practices—body scans, progressive muscle relaxation, and mindful stretching—are powerful tools for developing physical awareness and managing the physical effects of stress. By incorporating these techniques into daily life, individuals can become more attuned to their bodies, recognize the early signs of stress, and take steps to release tension and promote relaxation.

Healing Through Mind-Body Techniques

The connection between the mind and body is not only a source of stress and tension but also a powerful pathway for healing. Over the past few decades, research has demonstrated that mindfulness practices can help manage and heal various physical ailments, from chronic pain to high blood pressure. By addressing the mental and physical aspects of health, mind-body techniques offer a holistic approach to healing beyond traditional medical treatments.

One of the most well-researched areas where mindfulness has proven effective in managing chronic pain. Chronic pain is a complex condition that is often exacerbated by emotional factors such as stress, anxiety, and depression. Many individuals who suffer from chronic pain experience a cycle of physical discomfort and emotional distress, where pain triggers negative emotions, and those emotions, in turn, intensify the perception of pain. Mindfulness breaks this cycle by helping individuals develop a different relationship with their pain.

Mindfulness-Based Stress Reduction (MBSR), developed by Jon Kabat-Zinn, is particularly effective in managing chronic pain. MBSR teaches individuals to observe their pain non-judgmentally, without trying to resist or control it. By shifting their focus from trying to eliminate pain to simply observing it, individuals can reduce the emotional suffering associated with pain. Research has shown that MBSR can significantly reduce pain intensity and improve quality of life for individuals with chronic pain conditions such as fibromyalgia, arthritis, and back pain (Grossman et al., 2007).

Mindfulness also profoundly impacts cardiovascular health, particularly in lowering blood pressure and reducing the risk of heart disease. Chronic stress is a significant risk factor for hypertension and heart disease, as it leads to elevated levels of stress hormones like cortisol and adrenaline, which increase heart rate and blood pressure. Mindfulness practices such as meditation and deep breathing have been shown to activate the body's parasympathetic nervous system, which promotes relaxation and lowers blood pressure (Park & Han, 2017).

In one study, individuals who participated in an eight-week mindfulness meditation program experienced significant reductions in systolic and diastolic blood pressure compared to a control group (Hughes et al., 2013). The relaxation response induced by mindfulness lowers blood pressure and reduces the production of stress hormones, leading to better heart health over time.

Mind-body techniques are also being used to address immune system functioning. Chronic stress weakens the immune system, making individuals more susceptible to infections and illnesses. However, mindfulness practices have been shown to boost immune function by reducing stress and promoting relaxation. In one study, participants who engaged in mindfulness meditation showed increased activity in immune cells, suggesting that mindfulness can enhance the body's ability to fight illness (Davidson et al., 2003).

Furthermore, mindfulness has been used to support individuals dealing with autoimmune diseases such as rheumatoid arthritis and multiple sclerosis. Stress often worsens these conditions, triggering flare-ups and exacerbated symptoms. Mindfulness helps individuals manage the emotional stress accompanying these conditions, reducing the frequency and severity of flare-ups and improving overall quality of life.

Mindfulness offers a powerful tool for healing by addressing both the mental and physical dimensions of health. Whether managing chronic pain, lowering blood pressure, or boosting immune function, mind-body techniques provide a holistic approach to health that complements traditional medical treatments.

To better understand the healing power of mindfulness and the mind-body connection, examining real-life examples of individuals who have successfully used these techniques to manage physical ailments and improve their overall well-being is helpful. The following case studies illustrate how mindfulness practices have been applied in various contexts, from chronic pain management to stress reduction in the workplace.

Case Study 1: Managing Chronic Pain with Mindfulness

Darina, a 45-year-old woman with fibromyalgia, had been living with chronic pain for over a decade. Despite trying numerous medications and physical therapies, her pain persisted, leaving her frustrated and exhausted. After attending an MBSR program, Darina learned to observe her pain without judgment and to let go of the constant struggle to eliminate it. Over time, she noticed a significant reduction in her pain levels and an improvement in her emotional well-being. Darina's case demonstrates how mindfulness can change one's relationship with pain, reducing its emotional impact and leading to a better quality of life.

Case Study 2: Reducing Workplace Stress with Mindfulness

John, a 37-year-old project manager, had been experiencing high-stress levels due to his job demands. He frequently suffered from headaches, insomnia, and digestive issues, which he attributed to his work-related stress. After his company introduced a mindfulness program, John began practicing mindfulness meditation for 10 minutes each day. Within a few weeks, he noticed a reduction in his stress levels and an improvement in his ability to focus. John's case highlights the effectiveness of mindfulness in managing workplace stress and its positive impact on physical and mental health.

Case Study 3: Lowering Blood Pressure with Mindfulness

Maria, a 55-year-old woman with hypertension, had been struggling to control her blood pressure despite taking medication. Her doctor recommended that she try mindfulness meditation to help manage her stress. After participating in a mindfulness program, Maria's blood pressure decreased, and she could reduce her medication dosage. Maria's case illustrates the role of mindfulness in promoting cardiovascular health and its potential to complement traditional medical treatments.

These case studies show the wide range of applications of mindfulness in addressing physical health issues. Whether used for chronic pain, stress management, or cardiovascular health, mindfulness is valuable for promoting physical and emotional well-being.

Reflection and Personal Practice

As we conclude this chapter on the mind-body connection, it is essential to reflect on how we can apply these insights in our daily lives. The practices and techniques discussed in this chapter—mindful breathing, body scans, progressive muscle relaxation, and mindful stretching—offer practical ways to cultivate physical awareness and reduce the negative impact of stress on the body.

Consider starting with a simple body scan or mindful breathing exercise to incorporate these practices into your life. Set aside a few minutes each day to focus on your breath or to observe sensations in your body. As you develop a greater awareness of your physical state, you will become more attuned to the early signs of stress and tension, allowing you to take proactive steps to manage them before they escalate.

Additionally, journaling can be a helpful tool for reflecting on the current state of your mind-body connection. Consider the following prompts to guide your reflection:

- Where do I typically hold tension in my body?
- How does my body respond to stress, and what physical symptoms do I notice?
- What mindfulness practices have helped me become more aware of my body, and how can I incorporate them into my daily routine?

Regularly engaging in mindfulness practices and reflecting on your mind-body connection can cultivate a more profound sense of physical awareness and emotional resilience. This holistic approach to health will help you manage stress and promote long-term well-being and vitality.

As we continue this journey, remember that mindfulness is a practice, and its benefits unfold over time. By incorporating mindfulness into your daily life, you can develop a greater awareness of your physical state, reduce the negative impact of stress, and cultivate a more profound sense of balance and well-being.

References:

- Davidson, R. J., et al. (2003). Alterations in brain and immune function produced by mindfulness meditation. *Psychosomatic Medicine*, 65(4), 564–570.
- Grossman, P., et al. (2007). Mindfulness-based stress reduction and health benefits. *Journal of Psychosomatic Research*, 62(2), 175–190.
- Hughes, J. W., et al. (2013). Effect of mindfulness-based stress reduction on blood pressure: A systematic review.

Psychosomatic Medicine, 75(3), 212–221.

- Kabat-Zinn, J. (1990). *Whole Catastrophe Living: Using the Wisdom of Your Body and Mind to Face Stress, Pain, and Illness.* Delacorte Press.
- Park, S. H., & Han, K. S. (2017). Blood pressure response to meditation and relaxation: A meta-analysis. *Journal of Psychosomatic Research*, 99, 157–165.

CHAPTER 3: THE BREATH: YOUR ANCHOR TO THE PRESENT

Introduction to Breath Awareness

While often overlooked, breath awareness is one of the most potent tools available in mindfulness practice. It is a foundational element connecting the mind and body and offers immediate access to the present moment. In the ancient traditions from which mindfulness originates, the breath is seen as a vital force, a gateway to self-awareness, inner peace, and clarity. In our modern world, where distractions are abundant, and the mind is constantly pulled in different directions, breath awareness offers a simple but profound way to return to the present, to the "here and now" (Kabat-Zinn, 1990).

Breath awareness is an intuitive practice because breathing is something we all do at every moment. However, it is often done unconsciously, and breathing can become shallow and irregular in times of stress or anxiety. By consciously focusing on the breath, individuals can regulate their breathing patterns, promote relaxation, and bring themselves back into balance (Brown & Gerbarg, 2005). This is particularly relevant in stressful situations, where shallow breathing and an accelerated heart rate often exacerbate anxiety and feelings of panic.

The power of breath awareness lies in its ability to calm the mind and shift the body's physiological response to stress. Breath is deeply connected to the autonomic nervous system. Through controlled breathing, individuals can engage the parasympathetic nervous system, also known as the "rest and digest" system, to counteract the stress response triggered by the sympathetic nervous system (Jerath et al., 2006). Thus, breath awareness can help regulate emotional states, reduce stress, and improve mental clarity by encouraging mindful engagement with the body's natural rhythms.

Moreover, breath awareness serves as a powerful anchor to the present moment. In mindfulness practice, the breath is always used as a reference point, a constant that the mind can return to whenever it becomes distracted. One can observe thoughts and emotions without becoming entangled by focusing on the breath. This practice teaches the mind to let go of future anxieties and past regrets, offering a more centered, balanced approach to life (Kabat-Zinn, 2003). In this sense, the breath becomes a sanctuary, providing calm amidst the chaos of modern life.

It is essential to start small and to make this practice a part of daily life. A few minutes of focused breath awareness can improve stress levels and emotional regulation. As mindfulness expert Tara Brach notes, "Our breath is always available to us as a refuge, a place of rest and renewal" (Brach, 2012). As you read this chapter, you will explore the physiological effects of breath awareness and various breathing techniques that can be integrated into your daily routine for mental, emotional, and physical well-being.

The Physiology of Breathing

Understanding the physiology behind breathing provides a

deeper appreciation of how it affects our mental and emotional states. Breathing is not just a passive process that keeps us alive; it plays a crucial role in regulating the autonomic nervous system, which controls many of our body's involuntary functions, including heart rate, digestion, and stress response. The autonomic nervous system is divided into two main branches: the sympathetic nervous system and the parasympathetic nervous system (Jerath et al., 2006).

The sympathetic nervous system is responsible for the "fight or flight" response. When we encounter stress or perceive a threat, the sympathetic nervous system triggers physiological changes designed to prepare the body for action. Heart rate increases, breathing becomes rapid and shallow, and stress hormones like adrenaline and cortisol flood the bloodstream. While this response is essential for survival in dangerous situations, prolonged activation of the sympathetic nervous system can lead to chronic stress, anxiety, and a range of physical health problems, including high blood pressure, heart disease, and weakened immune function (Sapolsky, 2004).

On the other hand, the parasympathetic nervous system promotes the "rest and digest" response, which helps the body return to a state of calm and recovery. Breathing is critical in activating the parasympathetic nervous system, mainly when we take deep, slow breaths. By consciously slowing down the breath, we can reverse the stress response and encourage the body to relax. This is why mindful breathing techniques effectively reduce stress and promote relaxation (Russo et al., 2017).

One of the most well-known physiological mechanisms behind mindful breathing is its ability to regulate the **Vagus Nerve**. The vagus nerve, which runs from the brainstem through the chest and into the abdomen, is a critical player in the parasympathetic nervous system. It helps to regulate heart rate, digestion, and other functions associated with relaxation and recovery. Slow, deep breathing stimulates the vagus nerve, which activates the parasympathetic nervous system and promotes a state of calm (Zaccaro et al., 2018).

Research has shown that individuals who practice mindful breathing regularly experience lower levels of cortisol, the stress hormone, and exhibit a more balanced autonomic nervous system response (Jerath et al., 2015). In addition to reducing stress, mindful breathing has been linked to improved cognitive functioning, emotional regulation, and even physical health outcomes such as lower blood pressure and enhanced immune function (Creswell, 2017).

These physiological effects of mindful breathing demonstrate the powerful connection between the mind and body. Taking control of our breath can influence our mental and emotional states and physical health. The breath is a direct pathway to regulating the autonomic nervous system, offering a natural and accessible way to manage stress and promote overall well-being.

Breathing Techniques

1. Box Breathing
Box breathing, or square breathing, is a simple yet effective technique that helps regulate the breath and promote a sense of calm. This technique involves inhaling, holding the breath, exhaling, and holding the breath again, each for an equal count of four. The regular rhythm of this technique helps balance the autonomic nervous system and reduces the stress response (Grover et al., 2016). Here is how to practice box breathing:

- Inhale deeply through your nose for a count of four.
- Hold your breath for a count of four.
- Exhale slowly through your mouth for a count of four.
- Hold your breath again for a count of four.
- Repeat this cycle for several rounds.

Box breathing is particularly effective when you must stay calm and focused, such as before a presentation or stressful meeting. Focusing on the breath and counting the seconds can bring your attention away from anxious thoughts and back to the present moment. This technique is widely used by individuals in high-stress professions, such as first responders and military personnel, to maintain composure under pressure (Grover et al., 2016).

2. Diaphragmatic Breathing

Diaphragmatic breathing, or belly breathing, involves engaging the diaphragm fully to take in more air and promote more profound relaxation. This technique is beneficial for managing chronic stress, improving lung function, and enhancing overall physical health (Ma et al., 2017). Here is how to practice diaphragmatic breathing:

- Sit or lie down in a comfortable position. Place one hand on your chest and the other on your belly.
- Inhale deeply through your nose, allowing your belly to rise as you fill your lungs with air. The hand on your belly should move up while the hand on your chest remains relatively still.
- Exhale slowly through your mouth, allowing your belly to fall as you release the air. Again, focus on keeping your chest still while your belly does most of the movement.
- Continue this cycle for 5–10 minutes, focusing on slow, controlled breaths.

Diaphragmatic breathing is an excellent technique for reducing chronic stress and promoting relaxation. Because it encourages deeper breathing, it helps oxygenate the body more effectively. It stimulates the parasympathetic nervous system, which in turn helps the body return to a state of balance and calm (Russo et al., 2017). It is beneficial for individuals who experience anxiety or difficulty sleeping.

3. Alternate Nostril Breathing (Nadi Shodhana)

Alternate nostril breathing, or Nadi Shodhana, is a traditional yogic practice that helps balance the left and right hemispheres of the brain, promote mental clarity, and calm the nervous system. This technique involves alternating between the left and right nostrils while breathing, which is believed to purify the body's energy channels (nadis) and promote physical and mental harmony (Sengupta, 2012). Here is how to practice alternate nostril breathing:

- Sit in a comfortable position with your spine straight and shoulders relaxed.
- Using your right thumb, close your right nostril.
- Inhale deeply through your left nostril.
- Close your left nostril with your ring finger, then release your right nostril and exhale through the right nostril.
- Inhale through the right nostril, then close it with your thumb and exhale through the left nostril.
- This completes one cycle. Repeat for 5–10 minutes, focusing on the rhythm of your breath.

Alternate nostril breathing is beneficial for calming the mind and balancing energy levels. It can be practiced at the start of the day to promote focus or before meditation to bring a sense of calm and balance. This practice is rooted in ancient yogic traditions and has been shown to promote relaxation and improve cognitive functioning (Sengupta, 2012).

By incorporating these breathing techniques into your daily life, you can begin to harness the power of mindful breathing to manage stress, improve focus, and enhance overall well-being. Each of these techniques offers a unique approach to regulating the breath, and you can experiment with them to find which one works best for you in different situations. Whether you are looking to calm your mind before a big meeting, reduce anxiety in a moment of stress, or cultivate a greater sense of presence, mindful breathing provides a powerful tool for transformation.

References

- Brach, T. (2012). *Radical Acceptance: Embracing Your Life With the Heart of a Buddha*. Bantam.
- Brown, R. P., & Gerbarg, P. L. (2005). Sudarshan Kriya yogic breathing in the treatment of stress, anxiety, and depression: Part I—neurophysiologic model. *Journal of Alternative and Complementary Medicine*, 11(1), 189-201.
- Creswell, J. D. (2017). Mindfulness interventions. *Annual Review of Psychology*, 68, 491-516.
- Grover, S., Gaur, M., & Harde, P. (2016). Effect of 'box breathing' on stress levels and performance among medical students. *Indian Journal of Psychiatry*, 58(6), 329–333.
- Jerath, R., Edry, J. W., Barnes, V. A., & Jerath, V. (2006). Physiology of long pranayamic breathing: Neural respiratory elements may provide a mechanism that explains how slow breathing shifts the autonomic nervous system. *Medical Hypotheses*, 67(3), 566-571.
- Ma, X., Yue, Z. Q., Gong, Z. Q., Zhang, H., Duan, N. Y., Shi, Y. T., ... & Li, Y. F. (2017). The effect of diaphragmatic breathing on attention, negative affect, and stress in healthy adults. *Frontiers in Psychology*, 8, 874.
- Russo, M. A., Santarelli, D. M., & O'Rourke, D. (2017).

The physiological effects of slow breathing in a healthy human. *Breathe*, 13(4), 298–309.

- Sengupta, P. (2012). Health impacts of yoga and pranayama: A state-of-the-art review. *International Journal of Preventive Medicine*, 3(7), 444–458.
- Zaccaro, A., Piarulli, A., Laurino, M., Men

CHAPTER 4: RECLAIMING TIME FOR STILLNESS

The Importance of Stillness in a Busy World

In today's world, the demand for productivity and constant connectivity has made the pursuit of stillness more challenging than ever before. Between the persistent notifications from smartphones, the increasing workloads at jobs, and the pressures of social obligations, many individuals feel like they are always "on." This busyness culture, often glorified as a sign of success, overlooks its detrimental impact on mental health, creativity, and overall well-being. According to research by Harvard Business Review, constant busyness can lead to cognitive overload, diminishing creativity and problem-solving capabilities (Cross et al., 2016).

Stillness is not just the absence of movement; it is the practice of pausing amidst the chaos to cultivate inner peace and mindfulness. It is about allowing the mind to settle, reflect, and reconnect with the present moment. The concept of stillness is deeply embedded in ancient philosophies like Stoicism and Buddhist teachings, which stress the importance of mental clarity and self-awareness. Seneca, a prominent Stoic philosopher, once wrote, "To be everywhere is to be nowhere," highlighting that without moments of pause and focus, one cannot truly engage in life (Seneca, Letters to Lucilius).

In the modern context, this resonates more than ever. The constant barrage of information makes it difficult to focus, draining our mental energy. Stillness offers an antidote to this overstimulation, providing the mental space needed to think, make better decisions, and restore emotional balance. It is in these quiet moments that creativity often flourishes. For example, many innovators, from Steve Jobs to Bill Gates, have attributed periods of reflection and stillness to some of their most creative insights. Neuroscientific research also supports this, with studies indicating that moments of rest and relaxation allow the brain's default mode network (DMN) to activate, promoting creative thinking and problem-solving (Raichle, 2015).

Stillness is not just about mental well-being but also about physical health. Chronic stress, often exacerbated by constant activity and lack of rest, has been linked to numerous health issues, including cardiovascular diseases, weakened immune function, and increased susceptibility to mental health disorders like anxiety and depression (Cohen et al., 2007). Stillness, in the form of mindfulness or meditation, has been shown to reduce these risks by lowering cortisol levels, the hormone associated with stress (Tang et al., 2007). Therefore, making time for stillness is not a luxury but a necessity for maintaining mental and physical health.

Creating Morning and Evening Rituals

One of the most effective ways to cultivate stillness is by incorporating mindful rituals into your daily routine, specifically in the morning and evening. These rituals do not need to be elaborate; instead, they should serve as intentional moments to ground yourself and set the tone for your day or evening. Research has shown that structured routines help reduce stress by providing a sense of predictability and control in an otherwise chaotic environment (Kahneman, 2011).

Morning rituals are potent because they frame the rest of the day. Starting the day with intentional practice, rather than jumping straight into emails or social media, allows you to begin with clarity and focus. One such practice is gratitude journaling. By writing down three things you are grateful for, you shift your mindset towards positivity and abundance rather than stress and scarcity. A study published in the Journal of Positive Psychology found that practicing gratitude regularly leads to improved emotional well-being, greater life satisfaction, and decreased stress (Wood et al., 2010).

Another beneficial morning ritual is mindful stretching or yoga. These practices help you reconnect with your body and breathe, grounding you before the day's responsibilities take over. Research suggests that practicing mindful movement in the morning can increase alertness, improve mood, and enhance cognitive function throughout the day (Schmalzl et al., 2015).

On the other hand, evening rituals are essential for winding down and letting go of the day's stresses. Reflecting on the day's events without judgment through journaling or quiet contemplation can help you process emotions and prepare for restful sleep. Studies show that people who engage in reflective practices before bed tend to have better sleep quality and experience fewer symptoms of insomnia (Harvey et al., 2005).

One effective evening practice is a mindful breathing exercise. Taking ten minutes to focus on deep, slow breaths signals to your nervous system that it is time to relax, activating the parasympathetic response, which counters the effects of stress (Brown & Gerbarg, 2005). This helps reduce the overproduction of cortisol and allows the body to prepare for rest.

Mindful Pauses During the Workday

The workplace is often where the need for stillness is most acute. The modern professional environment can feel overwhelming with tight deadlines, constant emails, and back-to-back meetings. However, taking mindful pauses throughout the day can help alleviate some of this stress. Research from the American Psychological Association (APA) shows that incorporating short breaks into the workday increases productivity and decreases burnout (APA, 2019).

A mindful pause can be as simple as stepping away from your desk for five minutes to focus on your breath or take a short walk. This pause does not just allow your mind to rest; it also helps restore your focus and mental clarity. Studies have shown that short breaks improve cognitive function by allowing the brain to reset, reducing mental fatigue (Ariga & Lleras, 2011). These mindful breaks can significantly improve job performance and reduce errors, particularly in high-pressure environments where cognitive function is crucial.

Incorporating these pauses into your daily routine can be challenging, especially in fast-paced work environments where every minute counts. However, scheduling these breaks—just like you would any other meeting or appointment—ensures that they become a priority. Some professionals succeed in setting reminders or using apps designed to encourage regular mindfulness breaks. For example, apps like "Calm" or "Headspace" offer guided mindfulness sessions tailored to workplace environments.

In addition to personal well-being, these pauses can foster better colleague relationships. When individuals take time to reset, they are more likely to approach interpersonal interactions with patience and empathy. Research indicates that mindfulness practices in the workplace can improve team dynamics, reduce conflicts, and enhance emotional intelligence, leading to better collaboration and communication (Good et al., 2016).

Making time for stillness in a busy schedule may seem challenging, especially when life's demands pull us in different directions. Nevertheless, it is an essential practice for our well-being, and with thoughtful approaches, it can become a natural part of our daily routine. The modern world often glorifies busyness, pushing us to be constantly engaged, which can lead to exhaustion and burnout. Stillness allows for moments of reflection, stress relief, and clarity, fostering a more profound sense of balance and purpose. Here are several ways to effectively carve out time for stillness, even when life feels overwhelmingly busy.

Time-Blocking as a Pathway to Stillness

Time-blocking is one of the most practical strategies for embedding moments of stillness into a packed schedule. The principle is simple: dedicate specific blocks of time in your calendar to stillness, much like you would for a meeting, project, or workout. This could be 10 minutes for meditation in the morning or a 15-minute walk during lunch. Treat these times with the same respect and commitment you give to other appointments. Doing so ensures that moments of peace and mindfulness are a priority rather than an afterthought.

Research backs the effectiveness of time-blocking, especially regarding productivity and stress management. A study by Bailey (2016) highlighted that time-blocking helps individuals focus better on tasks and reduces the anxiety of juggling multiple responsibilities. It creates a clear structure in the day, providing periods of intense focus followed by necessary breaks. These breaks are an opportunity to cultivate stillness, offering time to recharge mentally and emotionally. By consistently scheduling and honoring these blocks, we prevent the overwhelm from a constantly packed, unstructured day.

Moreover, time-blocking helps establish a routine that includes stillness, making it a habit. Over time, these moments of stillness become something to look forward to rather than a chore. Whether it is a short pause to breathe deeply, reflect on gratitude, or sit quietly, this practice becomes valuable to one's overall well-being. As Bailey (2016) emphasizes, the key is consistency—just as we would not cancel an important meeting or deadline, we should resist the urge to skip these intentional moments of stillness.

Reducing Digital Distractions to Reclaim Time

In today's digital era, one of the biggest obstacles to finding time for stillness is the sheer number of distractions at our fingertips. Smartphones, social media, emails, and endless notifications fragment our attention and consume significant portions of our day. The problem is the time spent on these platforms and the mental clutter they create, which leaves little room for reflective stillness. As the saying goes, "Where attention goes, energy flows." If our attention is perpetually scattered across different apps and devices, our energy is depleted, and we are left with little bandwidth for quiet moments.

The extent of this distraction is staggering. According to a study by RescueTime (2019), the average person spends more than three hours per day on their phone, much of which is unproductive. When tallied over a week, this amounts to over 21 hours—time that could otherwise be dedicated to activities that bring stillness and fulfillment. While technology offers undeniable benefits, the key is to manage it in a way that does not interfere with our mental peace.

One way to reclaim this time is by reducing digital distractions through strategies like turning off non-essential notifications, using app blockers, and setting specific times for checking emails or social media. Engaging in a "digital detox" for even a few hours a day can free up time for reflection, relaxation, and mindfulness. Another effective strategy is setting clear boundaries around screen time. For instance, commit to turning off devices an hour before bed or schedule "tech-free" mornings where you begin the day without checking emails or social media. These small shifts can create pockets of stillness in the day, allowing for mental and emotional recovery.

By being intentional about our digital consumption, we recover lost time and cultivate a more transparent, focused mind. This reduction in mental clutter can lead to more significant moments of stillness, helping to ease the constant mental chatter that many of us experience. Research indicates that reducing digital distractions can improve our overall well-being, enhance concentration, and increase our capacity for reflection (RescueTime, 2019).

Reframing Time: Shifting the Mindset from "Busy" to "Present"

Another powerful approach to creating time for stillness is reframing our relationship with time. Too often, we equate being busy with being productive or successful. This cultural glorification of busyness can lead to feelings of guilt when we are not constantly "doing." However, as Levine (2007) points out, constant busyness can diminish productivity and lead to burnout over time. It is not about doing more; it is about doing what matters most and creating space for recovery, reflection, and renewal.

When we consciously prioritize stillness, we shift from a "busy" mindset to a "present" mindset. This shift involves recognizing that stillness is not a luxury but a necessity for sustained well-being and productivity. Instead of viewing moments of pause as wasted time, we can start seeing them as opportunities to reset, gain clarity, and connect more deeply with ourselves.

This reframing requires a mental shift from viewing our to-do lists as the measure of our self-worth. Instead, we can see time for stillness as an investment in our mental and emotional health. For example, try embracing moments of inactivity or silence rather than filling every spare moment with tasks. Waiting in line at a grocery store or sitting in traffic can transform into a mindfulness practice—simply breathing deeply, observing your surroundings, and being present. When reframed, these small pockets of time offer opportunities for stillness amidst the chaos.

Moreover, as Levine (2007) emphasizes, busyness often stems from a cultural belief that we are only valuable when we are producing. We can shift our priorities by reframing stillness as equally valuable—if not more so—than constant activity. Stillness becomes a powerful tool for maintaining balance, preventing burnout, and nurturing creativity and problem-solving skills.

Incorporating Stillness into Everyday Activities

In addition to setting aside time for stillness through time blocking and reducing distractions, another effective strategy is incorporating moments of stillness into everyday activities. Stillness does not always require long periods of meditation or isolation. If approached with intention and mindfulness, it can be found in the ordinary tasks of daily life.

For example, the next time you shower, instead of rushing through the process, take a moment to feel the warmth of the water, listen to the sound of the droplets, and focus on the sensation of the soap on your skin. This simple act of being fully present transforms a mundane task into an opportunity for mindfulness and stillness. Similarly, you can practice mindfulness while doing household chores like washing the dishes, cooking, or folding laundry. By focusing on the sensory experience of these activities—such as the texture of the clothes or the smell of the food—you create moments of calm and presence during your routine.

Walking can also be a powerful mindfulness practice. Instead of walking with a distracted mind or while scrolling through your phone, take a few minutes to observe your surroundings —the trees, the sky, the sound of your footsteps. This walking meditation helps you reconnect with your body and the present moment, allowing you to find stillness even in motion.

Incorporating stillness into these everyday tasks enhances your overall mindfulness practice and helps cultivate a sense of gratitude for the present moment. Instead of rushing through life's daily demands, you learn to find joy and peace in the ordinary. Over time, this practice fosters a more profound sense of contentment, helping you navigate the complexities of life with greater ease.

Building a Habit of Stillness: Starting Small and Being Consistent

The key to making stillness a regular part of your life is to start small and be consistent. It is easy to feel overwhelmed by the idea of finding time for stillness in a busy schedule but remember that stillness does not have to be a lengthy or complicated practice. Even five minutes of deep breathing, a short walk, or a quick pause to stretch can make a meaningful difference in your day.

The key is consistency, like any other habit; making time for stillness requires repetition and commitment. By starting small and gradually increasing the time you dedicate to stillness, you build a sustainable practice that fits seamlessly into your daily life. As with any new habit, there may be days when it feels challenging to pause or you are tempted to skip your moments of stillness. However, the benefits of regular stillness—such as reduced stress, increased clarity, and improved emotional resilience—will motivate you to continue.

To illustrate the transformative power of stillness, consider the story of Sarah, a lawyer working in a fast-paced corporate firm. For years, Sarah believed that success required non-stop work and constant availability. However, after experiencing burnout, she incorporated mindful pauses into her day, including a morning meditation routine and five-minute breathing exercises between meetings. Over time, Sarah significantly improved her mental clarity, productivity, and overall well-being. She also became more present in her relationships, no longer feeling the constant need to multitask.

Similarly, David, a father of two and a marketing executive, struggled to balance his demanding job and family life. By incorporating evening rituals, such as quiet reflection and gratitude journaling, David could create a space to unwind and reflect on his day. These practices improved his sleep quality and helped him feel more connected to his family and less overwhelmed by work.

Reflection exercises can help you identify areas where you can incorporate stillness. Consider the following journaling prompts:

1. What moments during the day feel most chaotic or stressful? How could you incorporate a mindful pause during these times?

2. Reflect on your current morning and evening routines. Are there opportunities to introduce stillness, such as a few minutes of meditation or mindful stretching?

3. How do you spend your free time? Could you reduce distractions like social media to make space for stillness?

These exercises encourage self-awareness and help you pinpoint areas where you can introduce quiet moments into your daily life.

Reclaiming time for stillness in a world that glorifies busyness is possible and essential for mental and physical well-being. By integrating mindful rituals, taking mindful pauses during the workday, and addressing common barriers to stillness, you can create a life that balances productivity with peace. Through structured morning and evening routines or brief moments of quiet throughout the day, stillness allows you to recharge, reflect, and live with greater intention and clarity.

References:

- American Psychological Association (APA). (2019). The importance of taking breaks. *American Psychological Association.*

- Ariga, A., & Lleras, A. (2011). Brief and rare mental breaks keep you focused: Deactivation and reactivation of task goals preempt vigilance decrements. *Cognition,* 118(3), 439-443.

- Bailey, C. (2016). *The Productivity Project: Accomplishing More by Managing Your Time, Attention, and Energy.*

Random House.

- Brown, R. P., & Gerbarg, P. L. (2005). Sudarshan Kriya yogic breathing treats stress, anxiety, and depression: Part II—clinical applications and guidelines. *Journal of Alternative and Complementary Medicine*, 11(4), 711-717.

- Cohen, S., Janicki-Deverts, D., & Miller, G. E. (2007). Psychological stress and disease. *JAMA*, 298(14), 1685-1687.

- Cross, R., Rebele, R., & Grant, A. (2016). Collaborative overload. *Harvard Business Review*.

- Good, D. J., Lyddy, C. J., Glomb, T. M., Bono, J. E., Brown, K. W., & Lazar, S. W. (2016). Contemplating mindfulness at work: An integrative review. *Journal of Management*, 42(1), 114-142.

- Harvey, A. G., Tang, N. K., & Browning, L. (2005). Cognitive approaches to insomnia. *Sleep Medicine Clinics*, 1(3), 383–399.

- Kahneman, D. (2011). *Thinking, Fast and Slow*. Farrar, Straus, and Giroux.

- Levine, R. (2007). *A Geography of Time: The Temporal Misadventures of a Social Psychologist*. Basic Books.

- Raichle, M. E. (2015). The brain's default mode network. *Annual Review of Neuroscience*, 38, 433-447.

- RescueTime. (2019). *The surprising stats behind how people spend their time at work.*

CHAPTER 5: CULTIVATING SELF-AWARENESS

Understanding Self-Awareness

Self-awareness, the ability to recognize and understand one's emotions, thoughts, and behaviors, is the foundation for personal growth and mindfulness. In today's fast-paced world filled with constant distractions, losing sight of our true selves can be easy. Self-awareness is about recognizing our emotions in the moment and understanding how they shape our reactions, decisions, and relationships.

The concept of self-awareness has long been explored in psychology. Daniel Goleman (1995), a pioneer in emotional intelligence, emphasizes that self-awareness is the cornerstone of emotional intelligence. We can only regulate our emotions effectively with the ability to observe and reflect on them. In contrast, self-awareness allows us to take ownership of our experiences without being overrun by automatic reactions or negative thought patterns.

In mindfulness practice, self-awareness is cultivated through focused attention. It enables individuals to observe their emotional responses, thoughts, and physical sensations without judgment or attachment. Jon Kabat-Zinn (2003), the creator of Mindfulness-Based Stress Reduction (MBSR), describes mindfulness as "paying attention, on purpose, in the present moment, and non-judgmentally." This approach encourages individuals to become conscious of their experiences as they unfold, creating space between stimuli and response, which is critical for emotional regulation and growth.

Self-awareness is the first step in creating lasting change. When we understand why we react in specific ways, we gain the power to choose our responses more consciously. For instance, someone aware of their tendency to react defensively when criticized can recognize this pattern and take steps to respond differently. Over time, this awareness fosters healthier relationships and better decision-making in personal and professional contexts.

The Role of Mindfulness in Enhancing Self-Awareness
Mindfulness strengthens self-awareness by encouraging individuals to tune into their internal and external experiences more clearly. Unlike reactive behavior, which is driven by automatic thought patterns, mindful awareness creates a gap between thought and action. Through consistent mindfulness practice, individuals become more attuned to their thoughts and emotions, allowing them to pause and choose how to respond rather than being swept away by emotional impulses.

A study by Farb et al. (2007) explored the effects of mindfulness meditation on brain activity, finding that regular mindfulness practice enhances self-referential processing. This means that mindfulness practitioners are better equipped to monitor their internal states without becoming overly identified with them. Individuals can develop a healthier relationship with themselves by recognizing emotions and thoughts as transient experiences rather than fixed aspects of one's identity.

Mindfulness-based techniques, such as meditation and mindful journaling, offer practical tools to deepen self-awareness.

Through meditation, individuals practice observing their thoughts and emotions without judgment, cultivating a sense of curiosity toward their inner world. Mindful journaling, on the other hand, provides a structured way to reflect on one's experiences. Individuals can gain insights into recurring patterns and underlying emotions by writing down thoughts, feelings, and reactions.

Furthermore, mindfulness promotes an attitude of self-compassion, which is integral to self-awareness. As Kristin Neff (2011) explains, self-compassion involves treating oneself with kindness during times of difficulty. Instead of criticizing or judging oneself harshly, self-compassion encourages individuals to acknowledge their challenges with understanding. This mindset fosters greater emotional resilience and allows for more honest self-reflection.

As individuals deepen their self-awareness through mindfulness, they become more skilled at recognizing emotional triggers, habitual thought patterns, and unconscious biases. Over time, this awareness leads to more intentional actions and choices, creating a pathway for personal growth and improved emotional well-being.

Emotional Intelligence and Self-Awareness

Emotional intelligence (EI), a concept popularized by Daniel Goleman (1995), refers to the ability to recognize, understand, and manage emotions in oneself and others. Self-awareness is the foundation of emotional intelligence, enabling individuals to identify their emotional states and understand how these emotions impact their behavior. Self-awareness makes it easier to regulate emotions or develop empathy for others effectively.

Mindfulness plays a crucial role in enhancing emotional intelligence. Through mindfulness practice, individuals learn to observe their emotions without being overwhelmed. Instead of reacting impulsively to challenging situations, mindfulness allows individuals to pause, reflect, and respond in a way that aligns with their values and intentions. This capacity for self-regulation is a crucial aspect of emotional intelligence.

Emotional check-ins, often used in mindfulness practice, can help individuals develop greater emotional awareness. This exercise involves pausing throughout the day to ask, "What am I feeling right now?" By regularly tuning into one's emotional state, individuals can become more attuned to the nuances of their emotions and recognize patterns that may otherwise go unnoticed. For example, someone may notice that they consistently feel anxious before meetings, indicating an underlying fear of judgment or failure.

Mindfulness also enhances empathy, another critical component of emotional intelligence. Empathy involves the ability to understand and share the feelings of others. By developing greater self-awareness, individuals become more attuned to their own emotions, which in turn allows them to understand the emotions of others better. Mindfulness encourages individuals to approach their emotions—and the emotions of others—with curiosity and compassion, fostering deeper connections and improved interpersonal relationships (Shapiro & Carlson, 2017).

Research supports the connection between mindfulness and emotional intelligence. A study by Schutte and Malouff (2011) found that mindfulness was positively correlated with emotional intelligence, particularly in areas related to emotional regulation and empathy. The researchers concluded that mindfulness training could enhance emotional intelligence by helping individuals develop greater awareness of their emotional states and more effective emotional management strategies.

As individuals cultivate self-awareness through mindfulness, they become more skilled at recognizing emotional triggers, managing stress, and responding empathetically in challenging situations. These skills are essential for personal and professional success, as they contribute to more effective communication, leadership, and decision-making.

Techniques for Improving Self-Awareness

While mindfulness is a powerful tool for enhancing self-awareness, specific techniques can be practiced to sharpen this skill. One of the most effective techniques is the body scan, a mindfulness exercise that involves bringing attention to different body parts. The body scan helps individuals become more aware of physical sensations and how they relate to emotional states. For example, someone may notice tension in their shoulders during a stressful situation, which can serve as a cue to take a deep breath and relax.

Thought tracking is another technique that can improve self-awareness. This exercise involves observing one's thoughts throughout the day and identifying recurring patterns, particularly negative or self-limiting beliefs. By becoming aware of these thought patterns, individuals can challenge and reframe them, leading to more positive and empowering thinking. For example, someone who frequently thinks, "I am not good enough," can replace this thought with a more realistic and compassionate statement, such as, "I am doing my best, and that is enough."

Self-compassion exercises are also valuable for improving self-awareness. As mentioned earlier, self-compassion involves treating oneself with kindness and understanding, especially during difficult times. One exercise that promotes self-compassion is the "Loving-Kindness Meditation," in which individuals silently repeat phrases of goodwill toward themselves, such as "May I be happy, may I be healthy, may I be at peace." This practice helps individuals develop a more compassionate and accepting attitude toward themselves, enhancing self-awareness.

These techniques can lead to profound self-awareness and emotional regulation shifts when practiced consistently. By becoming more attuned to their inner experiences, individuals can make more intentional choices, cultivate healthier relationships, and live authentically and purposefully.

Case Studies and Personal Stories

Real-world examples illustrate the transformative power of self-awareness and mindfulness. Consider the story of Jane, a corporate executive who struggled with chronic stress and burnout. Through mindfulness practice, Jane became more aware of the physical sensations associated with stress, such as tightness in her chest and shallow breathing. By recognizing these signs early, she could implement relaxation techniques, such as deep breathing and progressive muscle relaxation, to manage her stress before it becomes overwhelming.

Another example is Mark, a teacher who used mindfulness to improve student patience. Before practicing mindfulness, Mark often reacted impulsively to challenging behavior in the classroom. However, Mark developed greater self-awareness and emotional regulation through regular mindfulness meditation and emotional check-ins. He learned to pause before responding to difficult situations, allowing him to approach his students with greater empathy and understanding.

These case studies highlight how self-awareness can lead to healthier emotional responses and more effective decision-making. Self-awareness enables individuals to navigate challenges with greater clarity and resilience, whether in the workplace, at home, or in social interactions.

Reflection and Personal Practice

Engaging in regular reflection and personal practices is essential to cultivating deep self-awareness. These practices allow individuals better to understand their thoughts, emotions, and responses, leading to a more mindful and balanced life. One powerful exercise in developing self-awareness is journaling with a mindfulness prompt. For example, consider the prompt: *"Reflect on a recent situation where you felt overwhelmed. What thoughts or emotions were at play? How did you respond? How might you approach this situation differently next time using mindfulness?"*

This journaling exercise encourages a deep introspection into emotional experiences. Individuals can better understand their internal states by writing about the thoughts and emotions that arise in challenging moments. When overwhelmed, we often react impulsively or fall into automatic thought patterns —worrying about the future, dwelling on the past, or feeling disconnected from the present. Journaling helps to untangle these emotions, providing a space for reflection and growth. As you write, you may notice recurring themes in your responses, like a tendency to get anxious when facing tight deadlines or frustration when feeling misunderstood. This prompt explores past experiences and identifies opportunities for applying mindfulness in similar situations moving forward.

Mindfulness is the practice of being fully present in the moment and accepting one's thoughts and emotions without judgment. By applying mindfulness to emotionally charged situations, individuals can create space between their emotions and reactions. Instead of immediately reacting to stress, anger, or frustration, mindfulness teaches us to pause, observe our emotions, and choose a more thoughtful and intentional response. For example, next time you feel overwhelmed, you might practice mindfulness by taking a few deep breaths, grounding yourself in the present moment, and allowing the emotion to pass without escalating it. This allows for a calmer, more measured response.

Beyond journaling, incorporating mindfulness into daily life is vital to cultivating self-awareness. One simple yet powerful practice is daily meditation, mainly focusing on self-awareness. This type of meditation involves sitting quietly in a comfortable position, closing your eyes, and paying attention to your thoughts and emotions as they arise. The goal is not to suppress or avoid thoughts but to observe them as they come and go without attachment or judgment. Imagine your thoughts as clouds pass through the sky—you notice them but do not hold onto them. This allows you to understand your habitual thought patterns better, such as how you react to stress, conflict, or uncertainty.

For instance, during meditation, you might notice that your mind tends to drift toward worries about work or unresolved conflicts with a friend. Instead of engaging with these thoughts, acknowledge them and gently bring your focus back to your breath or the sensations in your body. Over time, this practice helps you become more mindful in everyday situations. You start to notice when negative thought patterns arise during your day, and instead of reacting impulsively, you learn to step back, observe, and respond more mindfully.

An essential aspect of both journaling and meditation is the element of tracking progress. Self-awareness does not happen overnight; it is a gradual process that requires consistent reflection and practice. By keeping a mindfulness journal, individuals can track their emotional experiences and how their responses evolve. For example, you might notice that a situation that once made you extremely anxious now feels more manageable after applying mindfulness techniques. Tracking this progress allows you to see how mindfulness impacts your emotional well-being and where you may need to focus more attention.

Moreover, journaling can also help identify specific triggers that consistently evoke strong emotional reactions. Reviewing past journal entries may make patterns of emotional responses more apparent. For example, you may realize that certain types of feedback from colleagues make you feel defensive or that social situations with strangers cause discomfort. Recognizing these patterns is the first step in addressing them with greater self-awareness. You can then create a mindfulness action plan—strategies to employ when facing similar triggers in the future, such as practicing deep breathing, stepping away for a moment of meditation, or reframing your thoughts in a more positive light.

The act of reflection does not stop at identifying triggers or emotional patterns. Journaling also provides a space to set mindfulness goals and intentions. At the end of each reflection, individuals might ask themselves, *"What can I do differently next time?"* or *"How can I approach this situation with more compassion, patience, or awareness?"* These reflections guide future behavior, making mindfulness a living practice rather than a static exercise.

By developing self-awareness, individuals gain greater insight into their thoughts, emotions, and behaviors, allowing them to make more intentional choices and navigate life's challenges more easily. Through mindfulness practices such as meditation, journaling, and self-compassion exercises, individuals can deepen their self-awareness and cultivate a healthier relationship with themselves and others. As the stories and techniques presented in this chapter demonstrate, self-awareness is a powerful tool for personal transformation and a pathway to greater emotional resilience and well-being.

References:

- Goleman, D. (1995). *Emotional Intelligence: Why It Can*

Matter More Than IQ. Bantam Books.

- Kabat-Zinn, J. (2003). *Mindfulness-Based Stress Reduction (MBSR).* In Clinical Psychology: Science and Practice.
- Neff, K. D. (2011). *Self-Compassion: The Proven Power of Being Kind to Yourself.* William Morrow.
- Farb, N. A., Segal, Z. V., Mayberg, H., Bean, J., McKeon, D., Fatima, Z., & Anderson, A. K. (2007). Attending to the present: Mindfulness meditation reveals distinct neural modes of self-reference. *Social Cognitive and Affective Neuroscience,* 2(4), 313–322.
- Shapiro, S. L., & Carlson, L. E. (2017). *The Art and Science of Mindfulness: Integrating Mindfulness Into Psychology and the Helping Professions.* American Psychological Association.
- Schutte, N. S., & Malouff, J. M. (2011). Emotional intelligence mediates the relationship between mindfulness and subjective well-being. *Personality and Individual Differences,* 50(7), 1116-1119.
- Hölzel, B. K., Carmody, J., Vangel, M., Congleton, C., Yerramsetti, S. M., Gard, T., & Lazar, S. W. (2011). Mindfulness practice leads to increases in regional brain gray matter density. *Psychiatry Research: Neuroimaging,* 191(1), 36-43.
- Kabat-Zinn, J. (1990). *Whole Catastrophe Living: Using the Wisdom of Your Body and Mind to Face Stress, Pain, and Illness.* Delacorte Press.

CHAPTER 6: REFRAMING NEGATIVE THOUGHTS

Introduction to Cognitive Reframing

Negative thinking is a pervasive issue that many people face daily, and it can have profound effects on both mental and physical health. These negative thoughts often manifest as automatic, unhelpful mental narratives that distort reality and shape an individual's perception of themselves, others, and the world. Whether it is an underlying belief of "I am not good enough" or the constant fear that things will always go wrong, negative thinking can trap individuals in a cycle of stress, anxiety, and low self-esteem. This type of thinking often arises from cognitive distortions—irrational ways of processing information that lead individuals to view circumstances in an overly pessimistic or unrealistic manner. These distorted thoughts can skew our perceptions, causing us to focus disproportionately on the negative aspects of situations and diminishing our ability to see the positive.

Cognitive reframing, particularly when paired with mindfulness, offers a powerful method for breaking this cycle of negativity. Cognitive reframing involves deliberately changing the way we perceive negative thoughts. It is based on the idea that, instead of accepting these thoughts as facts, individuals can challenge them and replace them with more balanced, realistic interpretations. This process shifts the focus from unproductive negativity toward a more constructive, compassionate perspective, fostering a healthier mental outlook.

One of the fundamental principles of cognitive reframing is the recognition that thoughts are not facts. Thoughts are fleeting mental events influenced by emotions, past experiences, and personal biases. Because they are not objective truths, they can be questioned, altered, and reframed. People often assume that it must be true because they have a thought. For example, someone might think, *"I am a failure because I made a mistake at work,"* and accept this as an undeniable fact. However, cognitive reframing teaches that thoughts are subjective and malleable, not set in stone. When individuals recognize that their thoughts are not definitive truths, they gain the power to shift their perspective, allowing them to move from a place of negativity and self-criticism to one of positivity and self-compassion (Beck, 2011).

To illustrate, consider the cognitive distortion known as "all-or-nothing thinking," where individuals see situations in black-and-white terms. For instance, if people do not meet every goal they have set for the day, they might think, *"I am a complete failure."* Cognitive reframing encourages this individual to challenge the absoluteness of the thought. Is it true that missing a few tasks means total failure? Have there been successes, even if small, that went unacknowledged? By reframing this thought into a more balanced perspective, such as, *"I did not accomplish everything today, but I made progress, and tomorrow is another opportunity to try again,"* the individual shifts from self-defeating thinking to a mindset that fosters growth and resilience.

Mindfulness plays a crucial role in the practice of cognitive reframing. Mindfulness is being present and fully engaged at the moment without judgment or reactivity. It encourages individuals to become aware of their thoughts without immediately reacting, creating the space to pause and observe. This non-reactive stance is essential for cognitive reframing because it allows individuals to step back and view their thoughts more objectively. Instead of being swept away by negative thinking, mindfulness teaches us to observe our thoughts as transient mental events that come and go, which can then be evaluated more calmly and rationally.

Mindfulness helps cultivate a technique known as "cognitive defusion," which involves separating oneself from one's thoughts (Harris, 2019). Rather than being consumed by negative thinking, cognitive defusion teaches individuals to create distance between themselves and their thoughts. For example, instead of thinking, *"I am a failure,"* a person practicing cognitive defusion might say, *"I am having the thought that I am a failure."* This subtle shift in language creates psychological distance, allowing the person to see that the thought is just that—a thought, not an intrinsic truth about who they are. By disassociating from the negative thought, individuals can better analyze it objectively, determining whether it holds any validity or should be reframed into a more positive and balanced interpretation.

To illustrate how mindfulness and cognitive reframing work together, imagine a person who often experiences the automatic thought, *"I always fail at everything."* With mindfulness, this individual can learn to notice when this thought arises without immediately believing or reacting to it. Instead of letting the thought trigger a downward emotional spiral, they pause, acknowledge it as a mental event, and question its accuracy. Mindfulness provides the space needed to reflect: *Is it true that I always fail? Are there times when I have succeeded? What evidence is there to support or refute this belief?* By bringing mindfulness to this process, the individual can consciously reframe the thought into something more balanced and constructive, such as, *"While I have experienced failures, I have also had successes, and I can learn and grow from these experiences."*

Over time, the combined practice of mindfulness and cognitive reframing can significantly improve mental and emotional well-being. Negative thinking is not just an inconvenience—it has real consequences on mental and physical health. Studies show that chronic negative thinking can increase stress, which in turn weakens the immune system, disrupts sleep, and raises the risk of developing conditions like anxiety, depression, and cardiovascular disease. On the other hand, individuals who practice mindfulness and cognitive reframing tend to experience reduced stress, better emotional regulation, and improved resilience in the face of challenges. They are better equipped to handle difficulties with a balanced, constructive mindset, which promotes mental clarity and emotional stability.

In this chapter, we will explore the mechanics of negative thinking in more detail, examining how it affects mental and physical health. We will also delve into various mindfulness-based techniques for reframing negative thoughts. These techniques include mindfulness meditation, body scanning, and mindful journaling, which can help individuals become more aware of their thoughts, recognize cognitive distortions, and reframe negative thinking patterns into healthier, more compassionate perspectives. By practicing these techniques consistently, individuals can break free from the cycle of negativity and cultivate a more optimistic, empowered mindset.

The Impact of Negative Thinking

Negative thinking can have profound, long-lasting effects on mental and physical health, making it a central concern in both psychological and medical fields. Negative thoughts are often automatic, unconscious, and repetitive, shaping how individuals perceive themselves, their circumstances, and the world. While an occasional negative thought may be a natural response to life's challenges, habitual negative thinking creates a harmful cycle that fosters anxiety, depression, and chronic stress. This cycle of self-doubt, fear, and frustration not only impacts emotional well-being but can also lead to a distorted view of reality and lower quality of life.

Over time, persistent negative thinking erodes self-esteem, promotes feelings of helplessness, and narrows one's perspective, making it difficult to appreciate the positive aspects of life. This mental pattern can act as a lens through which individuals interpret their experiences, often magnifying minor setbacks or disappointments and turning them into overwhelming problems. For example, someone might internalize a single criticism at work as evidence of incompetence or view a temporary setback as a sign that they are destined for failure. As a result, they may avoid taking risks, trying new things, or engaging with others out of fear of further negative experiences. In this way, negative thinking becomes self-reinforcing, limiting personal growth and contributing to stagnation and dissatisfaction (Burns, 2014).

The neuroscience behind negative thinking reveals why breaking free from these patterns can be challenging. The brain is wired to prioritize negative stimuli over positive ones—a phenomenon known as the *negativity bias.* This bias evolved as a survival mechanism, helping early humans stay alert to potential dangers. However, in modern life, where survival threats are less prevalent, this bias can cause the brain to overemphasize negative experiences, making it harder to maintain a balanced perspective. Negative thought patterns activate the amygdala, the brain's emotional response center responsible for processing fear, anxiety, and stress. When recurring negative thoughts overstimulate the amygdala, it can trigger the body's stress response, releasing cortisol, the stress hormone. While cortisol helps the body cope with immediate threats, chronically elevated cortisol levels due to prolonged negative thinking can harm brain function and physical health (Davidson, 2015).

Chronic stress caused by the amygdala's overstimulation can impair the prefrontal cortex's functioning, which is the part of the brain responsible for higher-order thinking processes, such as decision-making, emotional regulation, and problem-solving. When the prefrontal cortex is compromised, individuals may struggle to manage their emotions, solve problems, or make rational decisions. This can lead to a feedback loop where negative thoughts become more challenging to control, fueling even greater emotional turmoil and reinforcing feelings of anxiety, anger, or sadness (Siegel, 2010). Over time, this continuous activation of the brain's stress response can wear down the brain's ability to function optimally, leaving individuals more vulnerable to mental health conditions like depression and anxiety disorders.

The impact of negative thinking is not limited to mental health; it also manifests in physical symptoms. The mind and body are deeply interconnected, and chronic negative thoughts can contribute to a host of physical ailments. Stress-related symptoms such as muscle tension, headaches, digestive issues, and insomnia are often linked to habitual negative thought patterns. For instance, when someone is constantly preoccupied with worry or self-criticism, their body remains in a state of heightened alertness, known as the "fight-or-flight" response. This prolonged stress response takes a toll on the body, leading to issues such as hypertension, chronic fatigue, and compromised immune function. Over time, chronic stress caused by negative thinking significantly increases the risk of developing more severe health problems, including heart disease, high blood pressure, and autoimmune disorders (Kabat-Zinn, 2013). The physical impact of negative thinking underscores the importance of addressing it early to prevent long-term damage to both the mind and body.

Fortunately, mindfulness offers a powerful pathway for breaking this harmful cycle of negative thinking. Mindfulness, which involves paying attention to the present moment without judgment, allows individuals to observe their thoughts from a distance rather than becoming entangled. When practicing mindfulness, individuals learn to recognize their negative thoughts as temporary mental events rather than as absolute truths. This ability to step back from negative thoughts reduces their emotional charge and gives individuals the mental space to respond more positively and constructively.

The core practice of mindfulness revolves around witnessing *one's thoughts*, which fosters cognitive defusion—the process of separating oneself from negative thoughts. By observing thoughts as they arise and pass, individuals can detach from them and gain the perspective to assess them objectively. For example, when someone practicing mindfulness notices a recurring negative thought like, *"I will never succeed,"* they can pause and observe it without immediately reacting. Instead of spiraling into self-doubt, they might ask themselves, *"Is this thought based on evidence, or is it an exaggerated response?"* This inquiry opens the door to cognitive reframing, where individuals can shift their thinking toward a more balanced and constructive perspective.

Research strongly supports the efficacy of mindfulness-based interventions for reducing the intensity and frequency of negative thinking. Studies show that mindfulness reduces activation in the amygdala and helps regulate the brain's stress response, leading to lower cortisol levels and a calmer mental state. Mindfulness also strengthens the prefrontal cortex, enhancing individuals' ability to regulate emotions, focus attention, and make thoughtful decisions. These brain changes translate into real-world benefits: People who practice mindfulness consistently report lower levels of stress, anxiety, and depression, as well as improved overall well-being (Baer, 2006). Moreover, mindfulness has been shown to reduce physical symptoms of stress, such as muscle tension and insomnia, and promote healthier lifestyle habits, such as improved sleep quality, better eating habits, and more consistent exercise routines.

Through mindfulness, individuals develop the ability to create space between their thoughts and emotional reactions, enabling them to challenge negative thinking patterns and reframe their perspective in a healthier, more constructive way. Staying back from negative thoughts, acknowledging them without judgment, and consciously choosing how to respond empowers individuals to break free from negativity. With practice, mindfulness can help individuals cultivate a more open, resilient, and compassionate mindset, even in the face of life's challenges.

As we delve deeper into the topic of negative thinking, it is essential to recognize that these patterns do not define who we are. They are simply habits of the mind, shaped by past experiences, conditioning, and emotional reactions. The good news is that mindfulness and cognitive reframing techniques can rewire these habits, reducing their influence on our well-being and restoring balance in our lives. In the following sections, we will explore additional strategies for cultivating mindfulness, including specific exercises and practices that can help individuals develop greater awareness of their thoughts, reduce the intensity of negative thinking, and promote a healthier, more positive mental outlook.

Mindfulness and Cognitive Behavioral Techniques

Mindfulness-Based Cognitive Therapy (MBCT) has gained

widespread recognition as a practical approach for managing negative thoughts, depression, anxiety, and other mental health challenges. By integrating mindfulness practices with core Cognitive Behavioral Therapy (CBT) principles, MBCT equips individuals with the tools to observe their thoughts nonjudgmentally, recognize cognitive distortions, and reframe their thinking patterns in healthier ways. Combining mindfulness and cognitive behavioral techniques offers a comprehensive, evidence-based approach to improving mental well-being by addressing the root causes of negative thinking (Segal et al., 2018).

The fundamental principle behind MBCT is that thoughts, predominantly harmful, are not intrinsic truths but transient mental events. Our minds constantly generate thoughts, and many arise automatically, shaped by past experiences, emotions, and biases. However, the human brain is prone to cognitive distortions—habitual, biased ways of thinking that can lead to inaccurate and overly negative interpretations of events. These distortions often go unnoticed, yet they contribute significantly to feelings of anxiety, stress, and low self-worth. MBCT helps individuals break free from these habitual patterns by teaching them to observe their thoughts mindfully without automatically accepting them as facts.

Common Cognitive Distortions in MBCT

Understanding cognitive distortions is critical to implementing MBCT successfully. These distortions are irrational ways of processing information that can cloud judgment and lead to exaggerated emotional responses. Some of the most common cognitive distortions that MBCT helps to address include:

- Catastrophizing is the tendency to expect the worst possible outcome, even in relatively minor situations. For example, someone might think, *"If I make a mistake during this presentation, my entire career will be ruined,"* even though a minor error is unlikely to have such drastic consequences. Catastrophizing amplifies anxiety and stress, making it difficult to approach challenges with a clear and calm mindset.

- Black-and-White Thinking (All-or-Nothing Thinking): This distortion involves viewing situations as good or bad, with no middle ground. Individuals who engage in black-and-white thinking may believe that anything less than perfection is a failure, leading to extreme emotional reactions and a distorted perception of events. For instance, someone might think, *"If I do not succeed at this task, it means I am completely incompetent."*

- Overgeneralization: Overgeneralization occurs when someone draws broad conclusions from a single event or a limited piece of evidence. For example, after failing one exam, a student might think, *"I am terrible at school and will never succeed academically,"* even though the evidence does not support this conclusion. Overgeneralization often leads to feelings of helplessness and low self-esteem.

- Personalization: This distortion involves blaming oneself for events outside one's control, often assuming excessive personal responsibility. For instance, if a team project fails, someone might think, *"It is all my fault that we did not succeed,"* even though multiple factors likely contributed to the outcome. Personalization can lead to unnecessary guilt and self-blame, further reinforcing negative thought patterns.

The Role of Mindfulness in Challenging Cognitive Distortions

By identifying these cognitive distortions, MBCT allows individuals to challenge their automatic negative thoughts and reframe them with more balanced, realistic perspectives. One of the central techniques used in MBCT is the *thought record,* a tool that helps individuals break down their negative thoughts, assess their validity, and reframe them. The thought record process involves several steps:

1. Identifying the Negative Thought: The first step is pinpointing the specific thought causing distress. For example, someone might think, *"I always mess up presentations."* It is crucial to capture the thought as accurately as possible to begin challenging it.

2. Recognizing the Cognitive Distortion: Next, the individual identifies which cognitive distortion is at play. In the example above, the distortion is *overgeneralization* because the individual makes a sweeping statement based on a few instances rather than considering the full scope of their experiences.

3. Assessing the Evidence: After identifying the distortion, the individual asks for evidence supporting or contradicting the thought. For instance, they might ask themselves, *"Have I messed up every presentation I have ever given?"* The goal is to challenge the validity of the thought by gathering objective evidence.

4. Reframing the Thought: Finally, the individual replaces the original thought with a more balanced and accurate perspective. The reframe might be, *"I have had successful presentations before, and even if I make mistakes, I can learn from them and improve."* This shift in thinking encourages self-compassion and resilience rather than reinforcing a negative self-image.

Mindfulness plays a critical role in this process by helping individuals develop the ability to observe their thoughts without being consumed by them. In MBCT, individuals are taught to approach their thoughts with curiosity and openness rather than judgment. By practicing mindfulness, individuals learn to distance themselves from their thoughts, viewing them as transient mental events rather than absolute truths. This practice of *cognitive defusion*—the ability to separate oneself from one's thoughts—enables individuals to challenge and reframe their negative thinking with greater objectivity and self-compassion (Harris, 2019).

Mindfulness Practices in MBCT

In addition to thought records, MBCT incorporates mindfulness practices designed to cultivate awareness of the present moment and reduce emotional reactivity. Some of the most common mindfulness exercises used in MBCT include:

- Mindful Breathing: This practice involves focusing on the breath and observing each inhale and exhale without trying to control or change it. Mindful breathing helps individuals ground themselves in the present moment and cultivate a sense of calm. It also serves as an anchor for the mind, helping to interrupt negative thought spirals by redirecting attention to the breath.
- Body Scan Meditation: The body scan is a guided meditation that systematically brings attention to different body parts, from the toes to the head. The goal is to observe any sensations—such as tension, warmth, or discomfort—without judgment. This practice promotes body awareness and helps individuals connect with their physical experiences, reducing stress and tension.
- Mindful Observation of Thoughts: In this exercise, individuals are encouraged to observe their thoughts as they arise without trying to suppress or change them. The key is to notice thoughts as fleeting mental events, much like watching clouds drift across the sky. By observing thoughts without becoming attached to them, individuals can distance themselves from their negative thinking patterns and develop a more neutral, objective perspective.
- Loving-Kindness Meditation (Metta): Loving-kindness meditation involves silently repeating phrases of goodwill and compassion, first directed toward oneself and then extended to others. This practice helps

individuals cultivate a sense of warmth, empathy, and self-compassion, which is especially important for those who struggle with negative self-talk and self-criticism.

The Effectiveness of MBCT

Research has demonstrated the effectiveness of MBCT in reducing symptoms of depression, anxiety, and stress. A landmark study conducted by Kuyken et al. (2016) found that MBCT significantly reduced the risk of depression relapse in individuals with recurrent depression. The study also found that MBCT improved emotional regulation and resilience, enabling individuals to manage negative thinking effectively. Combining mindfulness and cognitive restructuring allows individuals to approach their thoughts with greater clarity and self-awareness, reducing the emotional intensity of negative thoughts.

Another study by Segal, Williams, and Teasdale (2018) found that MBCT was as effective as antidepressant medication in preventing depression relapse, providing individuals with a non-pharmacological option for managing their mental health. This research highlights the long-term benefits of MBCT, particularly for individuals who prefer a holistic approach to mental health care.

In addition to its benefits for individuals with depression, MBCT is effective in reducing symptoms of anxiety. By teaching individuals to observe their anxious thoughts without becoming overwhelmed, MBCT promotes a more balanced, grounded response to stress. Mindfulness-based practices, such as mindful breathing and body scan meditation, help individuals stay present in the moment, reducing the tendency to catastrophize or engage in black-and-white thinking.

Mindfulness-Based Cognitive Therapy (MBCT) offers a powerful approach to managing negative thinking by combining the strengths of mindfulness and cognitive behavioral techniques. Through mindfulness practices, individuals learn to observe their thoughts nonjudgmentally, recognize cognitive distortions, and reframe their thinking patterns with greater self-compassion and objectivity. MBCT's focus on both mental and emotional awareness makes it an effective tool for reducing symptoms of depression, anxiety, and stress while promoting long-term emotional resilience. By integrating these practices into daily life, individuals can cultivate a healthier relationship with their thoughts and foster a more balanced, mindful approach to challenges.

Techniques for Reframing Negative Thoughts

Reframing negative thoughts requires a combination of mindfulness and practical techniques that can be consistently applied in everyday life. These techniques can help individuals create new mental habits emphasizing positivity, self-compassion, and resilience. Reframing involves consciously shifting from automatic, negative thought patterns to a more balanced, constructive perspective. This requires awareness and practice, but these mindfulness-based techniques help reshape how individuals approach their thoughts, emotions, and experiences over time.

Here are several mindfulness-based techniques that can aid in reframing negative thoughts and transforming the way individuals perceive themselves and their world:

1. Gratitude Practice

Gratitude is one of the most powerful antidotes to negative thinking. When individuals focus on what they are thankful for, they are less likely to dwell on what is going wrong. A growing body of research suggests that practicing gratitude can help rewire the brain to notice the positive aspects of life more efficiently, promoting a more optimistic outlook. Gratitude has been shown to enhance well-being, increase life satisfaction, and reduce symptoms of depression (Emmons & McCullough,

2003).

One simple yet effective gratitude practice involves writing down three things each day for which you are grateful. These can be small, everyday moments like coffee or conversing with friends. The key is to be consistent and intentional in your gratitude practice. Over time, this activity shifts focus away from the negative aspects of life and highlights the abundance of positive experiences that often go unnoticed.

For example, someone experiencing a stressful day at work might feel overwhelmed and focus on what went wrong. However, by engaging in a gratitude practice at the end of the day, they could redirect their attention to what went well, such as completing a challenging task or receiving support from a colleague. This shift in focus can reduce stress and create a more balanced perspective. Regularly practicing gratitude has increased resilience, helping individuals bounce back from adversity more quickly.

In addition to writing in a gratitude journal, individuals can incorporate gratitude into their mindfulness meditation practice by dedicating a few minutes each day to silently reflecting on the people, experiences, and opportunities they are grateful for. This deepens the impact of gratitude by cultivating an emotional connection to the positive aspects of life.

2. Mindful Visualization

Visualization is a technique that involves creating mental images of positive outcomes or desired experiences. It is advantageous in shifting negative thinking patterns, as the mind responds similarly to visualizations of real-life experiences. By visualizing success, individuals can calm their minds, reduce anxiety, and mentally rehearse optimistic scenarios, increasing confidence and emotional readiness for real-life challenges (Gould, 2013).

For example, if someone is anxious about an upcoming presentation, they might visualize themselves delivering it smoothly, feeling confident, and receiving positive feedback. By repeatedly visualizing this successful outcome, they create a mental rehearsal of the event, which reduces fear and builds self-assurance. Visualization helps prepare the mind for future events and interrupts negative thought loops by focusing on constructive, empowering possibilities.

Mindful visualization is often combined with relaxation techniques, such as deep breathing or progressive muscle relaxation, to help the individual enter a calm and focused state. Once in this state, the person can create vivid, detailed images of the desired outcome. The more senses involved in the visualization (e.g., seeing, hearing, feeling), the more influential the practice becomes.

For example, an athlete preparing for a competition might visualize themselves performing at their best, feeling solid and confident, and hearing the supportive cheers of the crowd. This mental rehearsal reduces performance anxiety and increases the likelihood of achieving the desired outcome by priming the brain for success.

3. Self-Compassion Exercises

Negative thinking is often tied to harsh self-criticism, where individuals judge themselves harshly for perceived mistakes or shortcomings. Self-compassion exercises are designed to counteract this tendency by fostering kindness and understanding toward oneself. Mindfulness encourages a shift from self-judgment to self-compassion, which involves treating oneself with the same care and empathy that one would offer a close friend.

One simple self-compassion exercise involves placing a hand on your heart, taking a few deep breaths, and silently saying, *"May*

I be kind to myself in this moment." This practice can be beneficial when negative self-talk arises, as it interrupts the cycle of self-criticism and replaces it with a more nurturing internal dialogue. Research by Neff (2011) shows that self-compassion is strongly associated with greater emotional resilience, lower levels of stress and depression, and overall well-being.

Another joint self-compassion exercise is known as *the self-compassion break.* When faced with a difficult moment or negative thought, individuals can follow these steps:

1. Acknowledge the difficulty: Recognize the pain or discomfort of the moment by saying to yourself, *"This is a moment of suffering."* This step fosters mindfulness by acknowledging the reality of the present experience without judgment.
2. Recognize shared humanity: Remember that suffering and imperfection are part of the human experience. Say, *"Suffering is a part of life. I am not alone in this."* This helps reduce feelings of isolation and self-blame.
3. *Offer kindness: Place a hand on your heart or make another soothing gesture, and silently say, "May I be kind to myself? May I give myself the compassion that I need?"*

This exercise helps to shift the focus from harsh self-criticism to a more compassionate and understanding perspective, fostering more excellent emotional balance and reducing the intensity of negative thoughts.

4. Flipping "What-If" Scenarios

Negative thinking often involves catastrophic "what-if" scenarios, where individuals imagine the worst possible outcome of a situation. For example, someone might think, *"What if I fail this project and lose my job?"* These catastrophic thoughts increase anxiety and can create a sense of dread that inhibits positive action. To reframe these thoughts, individuals can practice flipping the "what-if" into a positive possibility, such as, *"What if I succeed beyond my expectations?"*

By focusing on the positive outcomes, individuals shift their mental focus away from fear and toward opportunity. This simple technique can have a profound impact on reducing anxiety and opening the mind to more optimistic possibilities. Reframing the what-if scenario also encourages problem-solving, as individuals are more likely to take proactive steps when not paralyzed by fear.

For instance, someone preparing for a job interview might be caught in a loop of negative what-ifs: *"What if I cannot answer the questions?"* or *"What if they do not like me?"* By flipping these thoughts, they can instead think, *"What if I impress them with my knowledge?"* or *"What if this interview leads to a great opportunity?"* This shift in mindset helps reduce anxiety and builds confidence.

5. Grounding Exercises

Grounding exercises are techniques designed to bring attention to the present moment, helping individuals break free from rumination or anxious thought patterns. When caught in a cycle of negative thinking, individuals often become disconnected from the present, focusing instead on past regrets or future worries. Grounding techniques redirect attention to the present, reducing the intensity of negative thoughts and fostering mindfulness.

One effective grounding exercise is the *5-4-3-2-1 technique,* which involves engaging the five senses to reconnect with the present moment. The steps are as follows:

1. Notice five things you can see.
2. Notice four things you can touch.
3. Notice three things you can hear.
4. Notice two things you can smell.
5. Notice one thing you can taste.

Focusing on sensory input pulls attention away from racing thoughts and back to the present moment. This exercise can be practiced anywhere and anytime, making it a valuable tool for managing anxiety or stress. Its simplicity makes it accessible and can be beneficial during moments of emotional overwhelm.

Grounding exercises also help to create a sense of physical and emotional stability. When individuals are grounded in the present, they can better observe their thoughts without becoming consumed by them. This reduces the power of negative thoughts and makes it easier to reframe them in a more positive and balanced way (Siegel, 2010).

Case studies and personal stories offer powerful, real-life examples of how mindfulness and cognitive reframing can dramatically improve mental well-being, reduce stress, and foster emotional resilience. These stories highlight the challenges individuals face and illustrate the transformative potential of these practices in overcoming negative thinking and enhancing one's quality of life.

Sarah's Story: Overcoming Imposter Syndrome

Sarah, a 35-year-old marketing executive, had always excelled in her career. However, she constantly struggled with imposter syndrome—a persistent fear that she was not good enough and that her success was due to luck rather than skill. Despite earning promotions and recognition for her work, Sarah often felt like a fraud, convinced that her colleagues would eventually discover her "incompetence" and that she would lose everything she had worked for. This fear led to chronic anxiety and self-doubt, affecting her performance and increasing her stress levels.

Through mindfulness practice and cognitive reframing, Sarah began understanding the nature of her negative thoughts.

Her therapist introduced her to *self-compassion* exercises, encouraging her to treat herself with the same kindness and empathy she would offer to a close friend. When she felt overwhelmed by self-doubt, she practiced placing her hand on her heart, taking deep breaths, and saying, *"I am doing my best, and it is enough."* Over time, Sarah's self-compassion practice helped her cultivate more extraordinary kindness toward herself, softening the harsh inner critic that had dominated her thoughts.

In addition to mindfulness, Sarah learned to use *thought records* to challenge her negative beliefs. When she thought, *"I am not good enough, and I will fail,"* she followed the steps of the thought record to assess whether this belief was accurate. Sarah realized she had consistently received positive feedback from clients and colleagues and had a track record of successful projects. She reframed her thoughts to reflect a more balanced perspective: *"I have worked hard to achieve my success, and my accomplishments are well-deserved."* This cognitive shift allowed Sarah to reduce her anxiety at work, and she began to approach challenges with more confidence.

After several months of practicing mindfulness and cognitive reframing, Sarah noticed significant changes in her emotional state. She no longer felt consumed by imposter syndrome and could enjoy her accomplishments without the constant fear of being "exposed" as a fraud. The transformation in Sarah's thinking enabled her to build greater self-confidence, enhance her leadership skills, and reduce her work-related anxiety.

James' Story: Managing Anxiety and Stress as a Teacher

James, a high school teacher in his early 40s, had always been passionate about education, but over the years, the demands of the job had taken a toll on his mental and physical health. He often catastrophized about minor classroom issues, such as a student's disruptive behavior or a lesson plan that did not go as expected. These small challenges would spiral into more considerable anxieties: *"What if I am not cut out for teaching? What if I am failing my students?"* These worries kept James awake at night, leading to chronic insomnia, headaches, and muscle tension.

Feeling overwhelmed, James sought help and began practicing mindfulness. One of the first techniques he learned was *mindful breathing,* a simple practice that involved focusing on his breath to stay grounded in the present moment. Whenever James felt his anxiety rising—whether during a stressful day at school or while lying awake in bed at night—he turned to mindful breathing to calm his mind. By focusing on the sensation of each inhale and exhale, he could interrupt his anxious thoughts and reduce the emotional intensity of his worries.

James also found great value in using the *thought record* technique to challenge his catastrophic thinking. When he caught himself thinking, *"If this lesson does not go well, it means I am a bad teacher,"* James would write down the thought, identify the cognitive distortion (catastrophizing), and then gather evidence to assess its validity. He realized that his students were learning and progressing while not every lesson was perfect. By reframing the thought into something more constructive, such as, *"I can improve this lesson for next time, but one difficult class does not define my abilities as a teacher,"* James reduced his anxiety. He began to view challenges as opportunities for growth.

Over time, James developed a more balanced approach to teaching. Mindfulness allowed him to stay present in the classroom, responding to student behavior with patience rather than frustration. Cognitive reframing helped him manage his stress by challenging the unrealistic expectations he had set for himself. As a result, James's overall well-being improved: his sleep quality returned, his physical tension decreased, and he felt more energized and motivated in his role as a teacher.

Rachel's Story: Coping with Grief and Finding Acceptance

Rachel, a 50-year-old mother of two, was deeply affected by the loss of her husband in a car accident. In the months following his death, Rachel struggled with overwhelming grief, guilt, and sadness. She often blamed herself, thinking, *"If only I had been with him that day, maybe I could have prevented the accident."* This thought consumed her, leaving her feeling powerless and unable to move forward with her life.

A grief counselor introduced Rachel to mindfulness-based practices, allowing her to process her emotions more compassionately and present. One of the most helpful practices for Rachel was the *body scan meditation,* in which she learned to pay attention to the sensations in her body—such as tightness in her chest or tension in her neck—without judgment. By tuning into her physical experience of grief, Rachel began to release some of the emotional tension that had built up over time. The body scan helped her reconnect with herself, making space for her feelings of sadness rather than resisting or pushing them away.

Mindfulness also helped Rachel challenge her negative thoughts. With the guidance of her counselor, she used *cognitive reframing* to address her feelings of guilt. She began by acknowledging that her desire to change the past was understandable but not rooted. She could not have predicted or prevented the accident. Rachel started to replace her thoughts of self-blame with more compassionate statements, such as, *"I loved him deeply, and I did the best I could with the knowledge I had at the time."* This shift in thinking allowed Rachel to find a sense of peace and acceptance, though her grief remained an essential part of her healing journey.

Through her mindfulness practice, Rachel also learned the importance of *self-compassion* during intense sadness. When waves of grief hit her unexpectedly, she practiced placing her hand over her heart and saying, *"It is okay to feel this way. I am allowed to grieve, and I am allowed to heal."* These acts of self-kindness helped Rachel navigate her grief with more grace, reducing her feelings of isolation and self-judgment.

Though the loss of her husband will always be a part of her life, mindfulness, and cognitive reframing gave Rachel the tools to cope with her grief in healthier, more compassionate ways. She feels more connected to herself and is gradually rebuilding her life, finding moments of joy and connection with her children as she moves forward.

Michael's Story: Managing Depression with Mindfulness

Michael, a 28-year-old software developer, had been dealing with depression for several years. His negative thoughts often took the form of *all-or-nothing thinking,* where he viewed life events as successes or failures. For instance, when he struggled to meet a work deadline, Michael would think, *"I am completely incompetent. I will never succeed at anything."* These thoughts contributed to his hopelessness, and he found it difficult to motivate himself to act.

Michael's therapist introduced him to *Mindfulness-Based Cognitive Therapy (MBCT)* to manage his depression. In MBCT, Michael learned to approach his thoughts with curiosity rather than judgment. One technique that profoundly impacted him was the mindful observation of thoughts, where he practiced noticing his thoughts as they arise without getting caught up in them. Instead of believing the thought, *"I am a failure,"* Michael would label it as a thought and let it pass, much like a cloud moving across the sky.

By observing his thoughts rather than identifying with them, Michael experienced a sense of freedom from the weight of his depression. He realized that his thoughts were not always accurate reflections of reality—they were just mental events that came and went. This shift in perspective allowed him to challenge his all-or-nothing thinking more effectively. In addition to mindful observation, Michael found value in *gratitude practice* as part of his daily routine. Each night, he wrote down three things he was grateful for, even small ones, such as enjoying a good meal or finishing a task at work. This practice helped Michael rewire his brain to focus on the positive aspects of his life, gradually reducing his feelings of hopelessness.

Over time, mindfulness and cognitive reframing helped Michael manage his depression more effectively. While his depressive episodes did not disappear entirely, he was able to cope with them more healthily. He felt more in control of his mental state, and his overall quality of life improved.

The Power of Personal Transformation

These case studies highlight the transformative power of mindfulness and cognitive reframing in helping individuals overcome negative thinking and lead more fulfilling, less stressful lives. Whether dealing with imposter syndrome, anxiety, grief, or depression, mindfulness-based practices offer tools to challenge cognitive distortions, cultivate self-compassion, and foster emotional resilience. As these personal stories demonstrate, the journey toward mental well-being requires time, patience, and consistent practice, but the results can be profound. Through mindfulness and cognitive reframing, individuals can reshape their thoughts, reduce suffering, and develop a more profound sense of peace and acceptance.

As we conclude this chapter, it is essential to reflect on how the practice of cognitive reframing can be integrated into daily life to help transform negative thinking patterns. Cognitive reframing is not just a theoretical tool—it is a practical, everyday method anyone can use to shift their mindset and approach challenges with greater emotional resilience.

Combining cognitive reframing with mindfulness allows you to observe your thoughts from a more compassionate and nonjudgmental perspective, allowing for profound mental and emotional growth over time.

Step 1: Identifying Negative Thought Patterns

The first step in applying cognitive reframing is recognizing the negative thought patterns you experience frequently. These thoughts often appear as automatic mental scripts that arise in response to specific triggers. For example, you might notice that after receiving constructive feedback at work, you immediately think, *"I am terrible at my job, and I will never be good enough."* Alternatively, facing a challenging social situation, you may think, *"No one likes me. I am not interesting or fun to be around."* These thoughts are typically exaggerated and based on cognitive distortions rather than objective reality.

To begin the process of cognitive reframing, take a moment to reflect on a specific negative thought pattern you often encounter. Please write it down in a journal or a mindfulness notebook. By physically writing out the thought, you create a sense of distance between yourself and the thought, which helps in reframing. For example, if your recurring thought is, *"I am not good enough at my job,"* write this down exactly as it appears in your mind.

Once the thought is written, the next step is to assess it with a critical but compassionate lens.

Step 2: Assessing The Validity Of The Thought

After identifying the negative thought, the next step is to assess its validity. This involves asking yourself reflective questions that help you analyze whether the thought is based on facts or driven by fear, insecurity, or past experiences. Here are some helpful questions to guide your reflection:

- Is this thought based on objective facts, or do my emotions influence it?
- What evidence do I have to support this thought?
- Is there evidence that contradicts this thought?
- Am I engaging in cognitive distortions, such as catastrophizing, all-or-nothing thinking, or overgeneralization?
- How would I respond if a friend or loved one expressed this same thought? Would I view it the same way?

For example, if your thought is, *"I am not good enough at my job,"* consider the evidence that supports and contradicts this belief. You might initially believe that your mistakes or difficulties prove you are incompetent. However, upon further reflection, you might realize that you have received positive feedback from your colleagues or supervisors, completed projects, and continually learned new skills. This evidence challenges the original negative thought, revealing that it is not entirely based on fact.

Additionally, recognizing cognitive distortions in your thinking can help dismantle the negative belief. In the example above, the thought *"I am not good enough at my job"* could be overgeneralized, where you are making a sweeping statement based on isolated incidents. By identifying the distortion, you can see the thought for what it is: a mental habit rather than an accurate reflection of reality.

Step 3: Reframing The Thought

Once you have assessed the validity of the negative thought and recognized any cognitive distortions, the next step is to reframe the thought into a more balanced and compassionate perspective. Cognitive reframing does not mean simply replacing a negative thought with an unthinkingly optimistic one. Instead, it involves finding a more realistic, nuanced, and constructive way of thinking about the situation.

To reframe a negative thought, consider the following steps:

1. Acknowledge your emotions: It is important not to dismiss or invalidate them. Even if the thought is based on distortion, the emotions you feel responding to the thought are real. Begin by acknowledging how the thought makes you feel, whether anxious, frustrated, or self-critical.

2. Introduce self-compassion: Be compassionate toward yourself as you work through the reframing process. Instead of harshly criticizing yourself for having negative thoughts, approach yourself with kindness and understanding. Remind yourself that it is natural to experience self-doubt or fear and that everyone makes mistakes or faces challenges in their work and personal lives.

3. Find a more balanced perspective: Replace the original thought with a more balanced and fact-based statement. For example, if the original thought was, *"I'm not good enough at my job,"* a reframed thought could be, *"I'm learning and growing in my role, and it is okay to make mistakes along the way. I have had successes in the past, and I can continue to improve."* This new perspective acknowledges both your challenges and your growth potential.

Regularly practicing this reframing process can break free from deeply ingrained negative thinking patterns and develop a mindset more aligned with reality, self-compassion, and growth.

Step 4: Incorporating Mindfulness Into The Practice

Mindfulness is essential to cognitive reframing because it creates the mental space to observe your thoughts without immediately reacting. Mindfulness allows you to step back and notice the flow of thoughts, emotions, and physical sensations without getting swept up in them. This nonjudgmental awareness is the foundation for cognitive reframing, as it helps you recognize your thoughts as temporary mental events rather than absolute truths.

To incorporate mindfulness into your reframing practice, begin with a simple mindfulness meditation. Set aside 10 to 15 minutes daily to sit quietly and focus on your breath. As you breathe in and out, notice any thoughts that arise without trying to push them away or engage with them. If a negative thought appears, acknowledge it— *"Ah, there is a thought that I am not good enough at my job"*—and gently return your attention to your breath.

Observing your thoughts from a distance helps you develop cognitive defusion, a technique that separates you from your thoughts. Rather than identifying with the thought— *"I am not good enough"*—you begin to see it as just one of many possible interpretations of reality. This mindfulness practice creates the mental clarity needed for cognitive reframing.

Step 5: Journaling For Continued Reflection And Growth

Keeping a journal is a powerful way to track your progress with cognitive reframing and mindfulness. Each day, take a few moments to reflect on your thoughts, emotions, and experiences. Write down any negative thoughts you encounter and practice reframing them. Regularly recording your reflections lets you observe how your thought patterns evolve and celebrate your growth.

Here is an example of a simple journaling prompt to guide your practice:

- What negative thoughts did I experience today?
- How did this thought make me feel?
- What evidence supports or contradicts this thought?
- What cognitive distortions might be at play?
- How can I reframe this thought in a more balanced and compassionate way?

By revisiting your journal entries over time, you may notice that specific thought patterns become less frequent or intense. You might also recognize areas where you have developed greater emotional resilience and mental clarity. Journaling provides a concrete way to track your progress and keep yourself accountable in your mindfulness and cognitive reframing practice.

Step 6: Cultivating Emotional Resilience

You will likely notice increased emotional resilience as you continue integrating cognitive reframing and mindfulness into your life. Emotional resilience is the ability to adapt to stressful or challenging situations without becoming overwhelmed by negative emotions. Regularly practicing reframing and mindfulness, you develop the mental tools to respond to life's difficulties with greater calm, patience, and self-compassion.

For example, the next time you face a setback at work, instead of immediately falling into negative thought patterns like, *"I am a failure,"* you can pause, take a breath, and assess the situation from a more grounded perspective. You might acknowledge your disappointment while recognizing that setbacks are a normal part of life and an opportunity for growth. This shift in thinking allows you to approach challenges with more resilience and less emotional turmoil.

Building a Lifelong Practice

Cognitive reframing and mindfulness are not quick fixes—they are lifelong practices that require patience, commitment, and self-compassion. As you continue to engage with these techniques, you will develop a more balanced and positive relationship with your thoughts, emotions, and experiences. Over time, you will notice a gradual but profound shift in how you respond to negative thinking, leading to greater emotional resilience, mental clarity, and overall well-being.

By making cognitive reframing and mindfulness a regular part of your daily life, you are investing in your mental health and cultivating a mindset that supports growth, positivity, and inner peace. Whether dealing with stress at work, challenges in relationships, or personal insecurities, these practices provide a robust framework for navigating life's ups and downs with greater ease and compassion.

References:

- Baer, R. A. (2006). *Mindfulness-based treatment approaches: Clinician's guide to evidence base and applications*. Elsevier.
- Beck, A. T. (2011). *Cognitive therapy: Basics and beyond*. Guilford Press.
- Creswell, J. D. (2017). *Mindfulness interventions*. Annual Review of Psychology, 68, 491-516.
- Davidson, R. J. (2015). *The emotional life of your brain*. Penguin Group.
- Emmons, R. A., & McCullough, M. E. (2003). *Counting blessings versus burdens: An experimental investigation of gratitude and subjective well-being in daily life*. Journal of

Personality and Social Psychology, 84(2), 377–389.

- Gould, D. (2013). *Imagery and mental rehearsal in sport.* Research Quarterly for Exercise and Sport, 84(2), 377–390.
- Harris, R. (2019). *The happiness trap: How to stop struggling and start living.* Shambhala Publications.
- Kabat-Zinn, J. (2013). *Whole catastrophe living: Using the wisdom of your body and mind to face stress, pain, and illness.* Bantam.
- Kuyken, W., et al. (2016). *Effectiveness and cost-effectiveness of mindfulness-based cognitive therapy compared with maintenance antidepressant treatment in the prevention of depressive relapse or recurrence (PREVENT): A randomized controlled trial.* The Lancet, 386(9988), 63-73.
- Neff, K. D. (2011). *Self-compassion: Stop beating yourself up and leave insecurity behind.* HarperCollins.
- Siegel, D. J. (2010). *The mindful therapist: A clinician's guide to mindsight and neural integration.* W.W. Norton & Company.
- Segal, Z. V., Williams, J. M. G., & Teasdale, J. D. (2018). *Mindfulness-based cognitive therapy for depression.* Guilford Press.

CHAPTER 7: MINDFULNESS FOR STRESS MANAGEMENT

The Relationship Between Stress and Mindfulness

Stress is an inevitable part of life, and while it can serve as a motivating force in short bursts, prolonged stress poses significant risks to both mental and physical health. In our modern world, the pace of life, constant connectivity, and pressure to perform can lead to chronic stress, which has been linked to a range of health problems, including anxiety, depression, cardiovascular disease, digestive issues, and weakened immune function (Lazarus, 2006). Chronic stress not only affects our emotional state but can also lead to physical symptoms like fatigue, headaches, and even long-term illnesses such as hypertension and diabetes. Understanding how to manage stress effectively is essential for maintaining mental and physical well-being.

The body's natural stress response, or "fight-or-flight" response, is designed to protect us in dangerous situations by releasing hormones like adrenaline and cortisol. These hormones prepare the body to react quickly by increasing heart rate, diverting energy to muscles, and sharpening focus. While this response is helpful in short-term, high-pressure situations, such as avoiding a car accident, it becomes problematic when activated for prolonged periods. Chronic stress keeps the body alert, leading to an overproduction of cortisol, which can damage the brain and body over time. High cortisol levels have been linked to memory problems, weight gain, sleep disturbances, and impaired immune function (McEwen, 2007).

In today's fast-paced society, people are often bombarded with daily stressors— the pressure to meet work deadlines, manage family responsibilities, or deal with financial uncertainty. Many live in constant stress without realizing the toll it is taking on their health. Mindfulness, a powerful tool for stress management, plays a crucial role here. Mindfulness effectively breaks the cycle of chronic stress by teaching individuals to respond to stressors calmly, measured, and non-reactively.

Mindfulness is practicing paying attention to the present moment with full awareness and without judgment. It involves observing one's thoughts, feelings, and bodily sensations with curiosity and openness rather than reacting to them impulsively. By cultivating this mindful awareness, individuals can create a mental "pause" to respond to stressors more thoughtfully and with greater clarity. Instead of becoming overwhelmed by emotions or stuck in a loop of anxious thinking, mindfulness enables people to acknowledge their thoughts and feelings, accept them as part of their experience, and choose how to respond more skillfully.

Research has consistently shown the positive effects of mindfulness on stress reduction. One of the most well-documented benefits of mindfulness is its ability to lower cortisol levels, the hormone responsible for the body's stress response. In a study by Baer (2003), participants who practiced mindfulness meditation regularly demonstrated a significant reduction in cortisol levels, corresponding to reduced feelings of stress and anxiety. By disrupting the body's habitual stress response, mindfulness helps regulate emotions, promoting a calmer and more balanced mental state.

Mindfulness techniques such as meditation, deep breathing, and mindful walking can be powerful tools for interrupting the stress cycle. For example, during times of heightened stress—such as a difficult meeting at work or an argument with a loved one—practicing *mindful breathing* can help activate the parasympathetic nervous system, also known as the "rest and digest" system, which counters the fight-or-flight response. Deep breathing exercises, where individuals focus on taking slow, deliberate breaths, help lower heart rate and blood pressure, fostering a sense of calm and reducing the physical symptoms of stress.

Another practical mindfulness technique is *body scan meditation,* in which individuals bring attention to different parts of their bodies, noticing areas of tension or discomfort. This practice helps individuals become more attuned to their body's stress signals, allowing them to release tension before it escalates into more significant physical or emotional issues. By regularly practicing body scan meditation, individuals can develop a greater sense of physical awareness, which is valuable for managing stress-related symptoms, such as headaches or muscle tension, before they worsen.

Mindful walking is yet another effective way to manage stress. By focusing on the sensations of walking—the feel of your feet on the ground, the rhythm of your breath, and the sights and sounds around you—individuals can engage fully in the present moment, giving their minds a break from worrying or ruminating on future concerns. This practice helps cultivate a sense of mindfulness in motion, making it easier to carry the benefits of mindfulness into everyday activities.

One of the most significant contributions to mindfulness and stress reduction comes from Dr. Jon Kabat-Zinn, a pioneer in applying mindfulness to modern healthcare. In the late 1970s, Kabat-Zinn developed *Mindfulness-Based Stress Reduction (MBSR),* an eight-week program designed to help individuals manage chronic stress, pain, and illness through mindfulness practices. MBSR integrates various forms of mindfulness meditation, including mindful breathing, body scan, and gentle yoga, to help participants become more aware of their thoughts, emotions, and physical sensations in a non-judgmental way. Kabat-Zinn's groundbreaking work has been supported by extensive research demonstrating that MBSR reduces stress and improves overall mental and physical health by enhancing emotional regulation, increasing resilience to stress, and promoting greater mental clarity (Kabat-Zinn, 1990).

For example, in a study conducted by Grossman et al. (2004), participants who completed an MBSR program reported significant reductions in perceived stress and improved quality of life. The study also found that participants experienced lasting benefits, with many reporting reduced anxiety and depression, improved sleep, and a more remarkable ability to cope with the challenges of daily life. These findings highlight the transformative potential of mindfulness practices in reducing the harmful effects of chronic stress.

Moreover, mindfulness does not just address the symptoms of stress but targets the root causes by changing how individuals relate to their thoughts and emotions. Rather than trying to eliminate stress, mindfulness encourages individuals to accept it as a natural part of life while learning to respond healthily. This acceptance allows for greater emotional flexibility, enabling individuals to navigate life's challenges more efficiently and resiliently.

In addition to its benefits for mental health, mindfulness has been shown to improve physical health outcomes, particularly those related to stress-related conditions such as hypertension, heart disease, and immune dysfunction. For instance, Carlson et al. (2003) found that cancer patients who participated in an MBSR program experienced reduced psychological stress and improved immune function, highlighting the mind-body connection in managing stress.

How Stress Affects the Mind and Body

Stress triggers the body's "fight or flight" response, an evolutionary mechanism to protect us from immediate danger. This response is deeply embedded in our biology and was vital for our ancestors' survival when facing predators or life-threatening situations. When we perceive a threat, our body floods with stress hormones like adrenaline and cortisol, which prepare us to confront or flee the danger. These hormones cause physiological changes, including increased heart rate, heightened blood pressure, faster breathing, and sharpened alertness (Sapolsky, 2004). This response helps us react quickly to immediate threats in the short term. However, in today's modern world, many of the stressors we encounter are not life-threatening but are chronic and ongoing, such as work pressures, financial worries, or relationship conflicts. Unfortunately, the body's stress response does not distinguish between these daily stressors and actual life-threatening events.

Over time, chronic stress can lead to detrimental effects on both the mind and body. Unlike the occasional burst of adrenaline we might feel during a high-stakes situation, chronic stress keeps our stress response "on" for extended periods, causing wear and tear on the body. One of the primary effects of chronic stress is on cognitive functions. High cortisol levels, the body's primary stress hormone, can impair memory and concentration, making it challenging to stay focused on tasks and retain information. This is why, under stress, you might forget important details or feel mentally "foggy" when trying to think clearly.

Also, prolonged stress suppresses the immune system, making the body more vulnerable to infections and illnesses. Stress diverts resources away from the immune system to prioritize immediate survival, which can weaken the body's defenses over time. Research has shown that individuals under chronic stress are more likely to catch colds, experience slower wound healing, and develop conditions related to immune dysfunction, such as autoimmune disorders (McEwen, 2008).

Beyond cognitive impairment and immune system suppression, chronic stress can significantly impact mental health. Long-term exposure to stress increases the likelihood of developing mental health disorders such as anxiety and depression. For example, anxiety often stems from an overactive stress response system, where the brain becomes hypervigilant, constantly scanning for potential threats, even in safe environments. This persistent alertness can lead to chronic worry, irritability, and fatigue. Similarly, prolonged stress can deplete the brain's levels of neurotransmitters like serotonin, contributing to the onset of depression. People under chronic stress may feel overwhelmed, hopeless, and unable to find joy in daily activities.

Furthermore, the physiological consequences of stress can manifest as physical health problems. Stress increases the risk of developing cardiovascular diseases such as high blood pressure, heart attacks, and strokes. The constantly elevated heart rate and blood pressure place undue strain on the heart and blood vessels, leading to long-term damage. Chronic stress has also been linked to metabolic conditions like type 2 diabetes and obesity, as stress hormones encourage the body to store fat, especially in the abdominal area, which increases the risk of metabolic disorders (Cohen et al., 2012). In this way, the effects of stress ripple through the body, impacting nearly every system.

Research has shown that mindfulness practices can counteract these adverse effects by promoting relaxation and activating the parasympathetic nervous system—also known as the "rest and digest" system (Creswell, 2017). The parasympathetic system is the counterpart to the fight-or-flight response, encouraging the body to relax, repair, and restore. When we practice mindfulness, we intentionally shift our focus away from stressors and toward the present moment, allowing the body and mind to down-regulate the stress response. Activating the parasympathetic nervous system helps lower heart rate and blood pressure, reduce muscle tension, and encourage more profound, relaxed breathing. Over time, this calm state reduces physiological arousal associated with stress, helping individuals better regulate their emotions and maintain overall physical health.

Mindfulness impacts the neurobiology of the brain in several ways that are especially beneficial for stress management. One key area of the brain affected by mindfulness is the amygdala, the brain's emotional processing center responsible for detecting threats and triggering the stress response. Studies have shown that regular mindfulness practice reduces the activity and size of the amygdala, making it less reactive to stressors (Hölzel et al., 2011). This means that mindfulness helps reduce the intensity of emotional responses, allowing individuals to remain calm even in stressful situations.

At the same time, mindfulness strengthens connections in the prefrontal cortex, the part of the brain responsible for higher-order functions such as decision-making, emotional regulation, and impulse control. With regular mindfulness practice, individuals develop greater control over their emotional reactions, improving their ability to stay composed under pressure. This improved emotional regulation means that when a stressful event occurs, individuals are less likely to be swept away by feelings of fear or frustration and can respond more thoughtfully and effectively.

In addition to its effects on the amygdala and prefrontal cortex, mindfulness has increased gray matter density in brain regions associated with learning, memory, and empathy. This suggests that mindfulness helps reduce stress and enhances cognitive function and emotional intelligence, making individuals more adaptable and resilient in facing life's challenges.

Mindfulness can also help reverse the adverse effects of stress on physical health. By promoting relaxation, mindfulness reduces cortisol circulating in the body, which, in turn, helps lower blood pressure and inflammation. These changes can reduce the risk of developing stress-related health conditions such as hypertension, cardiovascular disease, and autoimmune disorders. Furthermore, mindfulness has been shown to improve sleep quality, which is crucial for recovery from the wear and tear caused by chronic stress. Individuals who practice mindfulness regularly report falling asleep more easily, experiencing more profound, restorative sleep, and feeling refreshed and rejuvenated.

Stress has far-reaching consequences for the mind and body, affecting everything from cognitive function and immune health to emotional well-being and physical fitness. Chronic stress can impair memory, weaken the immune system, and lead to mental health disorders like anxiety and depression. However, mindfulness offers a powerful counterbalance to stress by promoting relaxation, enhancing emotional regulation, and supporting better physical health. By altering the brain's response to stressors, mindfulness helps individuals manage stress more effectively and cultivate long-term resilience.

Mindfulness-Based Stress Reduction (MBSR)

Mindfulness-Based Stress Reduction (MBSR) is one of the most widely researched mindfulness programs for stress management. Developed by Dr. Jon Kabat-Zinn in 1979, MBSR integrates mindfulness meditation with body awareness to help individuals manage stress, pain, and illness. The program has been implemented in various settings, including hospitals, schools, and workplaces, and has proven effective in reducing stress and improving quality of life (Kabat-Zinn, 1990).

MBSR involves several mindfulness practices that cultivate present-moment awareness and reduce reactivity to stress. One essential technique is the body scan, where individuals systematically focus on different body parts, noticing any sensations without judgment. This practice helps individuals develop a deeper connection with their bodies and recognize areas of tension or discomfort caused by stress.

Another core practice of MBSR is sitting meditation, where

individuals sit comfortably and focus on their breath, thoughts, or bodily sensations. The goal is to observe these experiences without becoming attached or averse to them. Through this practice, individuals learn to acknowledge stress and discomfort without letting them dominate their mental state.

Mindful movement, such as yoga or tai chi, is also part of the MBSR program. These gentle movements help individuals become more aware of their bodies, improve physical flexibility, and release built-up tension from stress. Practicing mindful movement enhances the mind-body connection and encourages relaxation and calm (Creswell, 2017).

Research has shown that MBSR significantly reduces symptoms of anxiety, depression, and chronic pain while improving overall mental health and well-being. A study by Khoury et al. (2013) found that MBSR participants reported lower levels of stress, improved emotional regulation, and increased resilience in the face of life's challenges. This section will explore MBSR techniques in-depth, offering step-by-step guidance on incorporating them into daily life to manage stress effectively.

Mindfulness Practices for Everyday Stress

While MBSR offers a structured approach to mindfulness, individuals can also benefit from simple mindfulness practices that fit into their daily routines. These practices are designed to help individuals manage everyday stressors, such as work deadlines, family responsibilities, and unexpected challenges.

One practical practice is mindful breathing, where individuals focus on their breath to calm the mind and body. When faced with stress, taking a few deep breaths activates the parasympathetic nervous system, reducing the physiological symptoms of stress (Baer, 2003). Mindful breathing can be practiced anywhere—during a work break, before a meeting, or even while commuting.

Another helpful technique is mindful walking, where individuals pay attention to each step, noticing how their feet contact the ground and how their bodies move through space. This practice helps ground individuals in the present moment and provides a break from the constant stream of thoughts that often accompany stress.

For those who find themselves overwhelmed by work or household tasks, mindful pauses offer an opportunity to reset. Taking a five-minute break to meditate or sit in stillness can help individuals regain focus and reduce mental fatigue (Hölzel et al., 2011). These short pauses allow individuals to retreat from their stressors, creating space for reflection and emotional regulation.

Case Studies and Personal Stories

Case Study 1: Rebecca, the Corporate Executive

Rebecca, a senior executive at a fast-paced multinational corporation, struggled with overwhelming stress. Her role involved managing teams across multiple time zones, overseeing high-stakes projects, and meeting tight deadlines. Over time, this pressure began to affect her mental and physical health. She experienced chronic fatigue, anxiety, and frequent tension headaches. The constant demand for her attention left her feeling burned out, and she found it difficult to switch off from work, even during her time.

In search of a solution, Rebecca turned to mindfulness-based practices. She started small, incorporating 10-minute mindful breathing exercises into her daily routine each morning. As she became more comfortable with the practice, she extended her mindfulness sessions to include 20 minutes of meditation during lunch breaks and another session before bedtime. Rebecca also began practicing mindful walking during her commute, observing the sights and sounds around her without distraction.

Over a few months, she noticed significantly reduced her stress levels. She became better equipped to manage high-pressure situations like board meetings and looming project deadlines. Her ability to stay calm and focused improved, and she no longer reacted impulsively when under stress. Mindfulness helped Rebecca cultivate a sense of presence, allowing her to approach tasks with a clear and balanced mindset. In addition, Rebecca reported that mindfulness improved her work-life balance. She could disconnect from work after hours, sleep better, and enjoy her time with her family. Ultimately, mindfulness empowered her to take control of her stress and emotional responses, which enhanced her overall performance at work.

Case Study 2: Mark, the Healthcare Worker

Mark, a healthcare professional working in a high-stress hospital environment, experienced a different set of challenges. As a nurse on the front lines, he dealt with emotionally draining situations daily. The demands of caring for critically ill patients, coupled with long shifts, began to take a toll on his mental health. Mark started to feel emotionally exhausted, experiencing symptoms of burnout such as irritability, lack of motivation, and difficulty focusing. The emotional weight of constantly witnessing the patient's suffering and loss left him feeling depleted.

Feeling overwhelmed, Mark enrolled in an eight-week Mindfulness-Based Stress Reduction (MBSR) program. This program taught him several mindfulness techniques, including body scanning, mindful movement, and meditation. Mark discovered that body scans were beneficial for releasing built-up physical tension from long shifts. By bringing awareness to different body parts, he identified areas of tightness and consciously worked to relax them. This simple practice allowed him to reduce physical stress, improve his posture, and alleviate chronic back pain.

Mark also practiced mindful breathing during emotionally tricky moments, such as dealing with distressed family members or delivering difficult news to patients. Taking slow, deep breaths helped him stay grounded and present, enabling him to provide compassionate care without becoming overwhelmed by emotions. Over time, he noticed that his ability to manage stress improved, and he felt more emotionally resilient. Mark's mindfulness practice helped him avoid burnout and deepened his connection with his patients. By being fully present, he provided better care and established more robust relationships with those under his care.

Mark's experience illustrates how mindfulness can be crucial in healthcare, where stress and burnout occur daily. His story highlights the importance of self-care and the profound impact mindfulness can have on emotional and physical well-being in such demanding environments.

Case Study 3: Sarah, the Entrepreneur

Sarah, a small business owner running a startup, faced unique challenges. As the founder and CEO of a growing business, she had to wear many hats—handling product development, marketing, customer service, and finances. The pressure to succeed, coupled with the uncertainty of running a startup, led to sleepless nights, anxiety, and frequent bouts of self-doubt. Sarah often found herself ruminating on potential failures, affecting her ability to focus on the tasks.

After attending a mindfulness workshop tailored for entrepreneurs, Sarah began incorporating mindfulness practices into her routine. She used guided meditation apps to help her stay focused and present during hectic workdays. Whenever she felt overwhelmed, Sarah practiced mindful breathing to bring her attention back to the present moment. She also embraced the concept of non-judgment, learning to observe her thoughts without attaching negative labels to them. This shift in mindset helped Sarah stop second-guessing herself and focus on her accomplishments.

As a result, Sarah's productivity increased, and she found that she could make more transparent, more confident decisions. Mindfulness also allowed her to manage the stress of running a startup more effectively, giving her the mental space to innovate and grow her business. Her experience demonstrates the potential of mindfulness in entrepreneurship, where mental clarity and emotional resilience are critical to navigating uncertainty and fostering success.

Lessons Learned from These Case Studies

These case studies show that mindfulness is not a one-size-fits-all solution but a versatile practice that can be adapted to different circumstances. Whether working in a corporate office, a healthcare setting, or running your own business, mindfulness offers tools to manage stress, improve focus, and enhance emotional well-being. The key takeaway from these stories is that consistent mindfulness practice fosters resilience —an essential quality for navigating the challenges of high-stress environments.

Mindfulness teaches individuals to respond to stress with awareness rather than reactivity, enabling them to handle pressure more easily. Over time, this practice leads to improved mental clarity, emotional balance, and a more profound sense of fulfillment in both personal and professional life. The stories of Rebecca, Mark, and Sarah are potent reminders of mindfulness's transformative power in the modern world, where stress is often unavoidable. However, they can be managed with the right tools and mindset.

As we conclude this chapter, exploring how mindfulness can be seamlessly integrated into your personal stress management toolkit is essential. Mindfulness offers a pathway to managing stress and transforming your relationship with it. By reflecting on your current experiences with stress and adopting consistent mindfulness practices, you can cultivate greater emotional resilience, mental clarity, and a sense of inner peace.

Step 1: Assess Your Current Stress Levels

The first step in creating a mindfulness-based stress management plan is self-awareness. Begin by assessing your current stress levels. What are the most significant sources of stress in your life? For some, stress may stem from work-related responsibilities, such as tight deadlines, a heavy workload, or interpersonal conflicts with colleagues. For others, stress might arise from personal life challenges, such as family dynamics, financial concerns, or health issues. Identifying the root causes of stress allows you to understand where to focus your mindfulness practice.

Next, take a moment to reflect on how you typically respond to stress. Do you experience physical symptoms such as tension, headaches, or fatigue? Or do you notice more emotional responses, such as irritability, anxiety, or difficulty concentrating? Many people fall into patterns of reactivity, where their stress response is automatic and unexamined. By bringing awareness to these patterns, you can begin to interrupt the cycle of stress and choose more mindful ways of responding.

Step 2: Use A Stress Journal To Track Your Stressors

A stress journal is one of the most effective tools for building self-awareness around stress. A stress journal lets you track your stressors and responses to them over time, offering valuable insights into patterns and triggers. Each time you feel stressed, take a few moments to write down the situation, your emotional and physical response, and how you managed it. For example, you might note that a last-minute work assignment triggered anxiety and tension in your shoulders, leading you to react with frustration. By documenting these experiences, you record how stress manifests in your life.

Over time, you will notice patterns as you accumulate entries in your stress journal. You may find that your stress levels are highest during certain times of the day or when interacting with specific individuals. You might also observe how your typical stress responses—such as withdrawing, lashing out, or overthinking—affect your well-being. These observations can provide valuable clues about how mindfulness can help you regulate your reactions. The goal is not to eliminate stress but to develop more constructive ways of engaging with it.

Step 3: Incorporate Mindfulness Practices Into Your Daily Routine

Once you have gained insight into your stressors and responses, the next step is to incorporate mindfulness practices into your daily routine. Mindfulness is not a one-time fix but a consistent practice that builds resilience over time. Begin by setting aside 5–10 minutes daily for a guided mindfulness practice. This could include deep breathing exercises, body scans, or mindful meditation. Start your day with a mindful check-in, taking a few deep breaths, and setting an intention for how you want to approach any challenges ahead. You could also end your day with a body scan, focusing on areas of tension and consciously releasing it.

For example, focus on taking slow, deep breaths when practicing mindful breathing. Inhale through your nose for a count of four, hold your breath for four counts, and then exhale slowly through your mouth for four counts. This simple exercise helps activate the body's parasympathetic nervous system, which promotes relaxation and counteracts the fight-or-flight response of stress. Regularly engaging in mindful breathing builds your capacity to stay calm and centered, even in high-pressure situations.

Step 4: Build Emotional Resilience Through Mindfulness

Mindfulness helps you develop emotional resilience by teaching you to observe your emotions without getting swept away. One technique to enhance this skill is to practice noting, where you mentally label your emotions as they arise without judgment. For example, if you notice frustration or impatience during a stressful situation, note to yourself, "frustration is here" or "impatience is present." Labeling creates a space between you and the emotion, allowing you to respond thoughtfully rather than impulsively. Over time, you will become more adept at identifying your emotional states and regulating your responses.

Another practice for building emotional resilience is self-compassion meditation, which involves offering kindness and understanding to yourself in moments of difficulty. When you encounter a stressful situation, try placing your hand on your heart, taking a few deep breaths, and silently repeating, "May I be kind to myself in this moment." This practice reminds you that it is okay to experience stress and encourages you to treat yourself with the compassion you would offer a friend. By integrating self-compassion into your mindfulness practice, you can reduce the harsh self-criticism that often accompanies stress and cultivate a more supportive inner dialogue.

Step 5: Reframe Your Relationship With Stress

One of the critical insights mindfulness offers is that stress is not inherently harmful. Instead of viewing stress as something to be avoided or eliminated, mindfulness encourages you to see it as an opportunity for growth. With regular practice, you can reframe your relationship with stress, recognizing it as a natural part of life that can be managed skillfully. For example, when faced with a stressful situation, instead of thinking, "This is too much; I cannot handle it," you might reframe your thoughts to say, "This is challenging, but I have the tools to navigate it."

Mindfulness also teaches you to stay present with the discomfort of stress rather than rushing to avoid or escape it. By staying present, you build the capacity to endure difficult emotions without becoming overwhelmed. Over time, this practice helps you cultivate a more profound trust in navigating life's challenges with clarity and poise.

Step 6: Make Mindfulness A Habit For Long-Term Stress Management

The benefits of mindfulness are cumulative, meaning that the more consistently you practice, the greater your ability to manage stress will become. As you continue your mindfulness journey, consider expanding your practice to include different techniques, such as mindful walking, loving-kindness meditation, or visualization exercises. Mindful walking, for instance, allows you to bring your awareness to each step and the sensations of your body as you move. This practice can be beneficial during breaks at work, offering a moment of calm and grounding in the middle of a busy day.

Loving-kindness meditation involves sending well-wishes to yourself and others, promoting a sense of connection and compassion that can buffer against the isolating effects of stress. Visualization exercises, where you imagine yourself successfully handling a stressful situation, can also help build confidence and reduce anxiety.

Committing to these practices daily creates a foundation of inner calm that supports you in even the most challenging times. You will be more able to navigate life's ups and downs with equanimity and ease.

Step 7: Celebrate Your Progress And Growth

Finally, as you integrate mindfulness into your life, celebrate your progress. Recognize the small victories—responding calmly in a stressful situation, noticing tension in your body before it escalates, or taking a mindful pause before reacting. Each step forward in your mindfulness practice is a testament to your growth and resilience.

By incorporating mindfulness into your daily life, you can break the cycle of chronic stress and cultivate a lasting sense of inner peace and balance. Over time, you will develop greater emotional awareness, mental clarity, and the ability to navigate stress gracefully. Mindfulness empowers you to take control of your responses to stress, offering a pathway to a healthier, more fulfilling life.

References:

- Baer, R. A. (2003). Mindfulness training as a clinical intervention: A conceptual and empirical review. *Clinical Psychology: Science and Practice, 10*(2), 125–143.

- Cohen, S., Janicki-Deverts, D., & Miller, G. E. (2012). Psychological stress and disease. *JAMA, 298*(14), 1685-1687.

- Creswell, J. D. (2017). Mindfulness interventions. *Annual Review of Psychology, 68,* 491-516.

- Hölzel, B. K., Carmody, J., Vangel, M., Congleton, C., Yerramsetti, S. M., Gard, T., & Lazar, S. W. (2011). Mindfulness practice leads to increases in regional brain gray matter density. *Psychiatry Research: Neuroimaging, 191*(1), 36-43.

- Kabat-Zinn, J. (1990). *Whole Catastrophe Living: Using the Wisdom of Your Body and Mind to Face Stress, Pain, and Illness.* Delacorte Press.

- Khoury, B., Lecomte, T., Fortin, G., Masse, M., Therien, P., Bouchard, V., ... & Hofmann, S. G. (2013). Mindfulness-based therapy: A comprehensive meta-analysis. *Clinical Psychology Review, 33*(6), 763-771.

- McEwen, B. S. (2008). Central effects of stress hormones in health and disease: Understanding the protective and damaging effects of stress and stress mediators. *European Journal of Pharmacology, 583*(2-3), 174-185.

- Sapolsky, R. M. (2004). *Why Zebras Don't Get Ulcers.* Holt

Paperbacks.

CHAPTER 8: MINDFUL COMMUNICATION

The Importance of Mindful Communication

Communication is at the heart of human interaction, influencing every relationship we form, whether personal or professional. In the fast-paced digital age, conversations often become transactional or superficial, limited to brief information exchanges without deeper connection. However, mindful communication takes a different approach by emphasizing being fully present verbally, emotionally, and mentally in each conversation. Mindful communication involves engaging in dialogue where listening and speaking happen with awareness, focus, and empathy. By practicing mindful communication, we can improve the quality of our interactions, enhance understanding, and build stronger, more meaningful relationships.

At its core, mindful communication means listening without judgment and responding intentionally. Active listening involves entirely focusing on the speaker rather than formulating a response while talking or being distracted by external stimuli, such as checking a phone. When we listen mindfully, we tune into the speaker's words, tone, and body language to understand what is being said and the emotions and intentions behind the message. This presence creates a supportive space where the other person feels heard and valued. In turn, our responses become more thoughtful and considerate, reflecting the true intention behind the conversation.

In mindful communication, the goal is to convey a message and deeply connect with the other person, creating space for understanding and empathy. Psychologist Daniel Siegel (2010) describes mindful communication as involving awareness of our own internal experiences while attuning to the experiences of others. This dual awareness—of ourselves and the other person—enables us to communicate with greater compassion and insight. By bringing mindfulness into our conversations, we reduce misunderstandings, defensiveness, and reactive tendencies that often escalate into conflict or disconnection. For example, when we engage in a heated debate, mindful communication allows us to pause, recognize our emotional triggers, and respond with clarity rather than letting anger or frustration dictate our words.

The benefits of mindful communication extend beyond improving personal relationships. In the workplace, mindful communication enhances team collaboration, leadership, and productivity. Leaders who practice mindful communication can better connect with their employees, offering constructive and empathetic feedback. This fosters a positive work environment where team members feel respected and heard. Moreover, mindful communication in professional settings leads to more effective problem-solving and decision-making. Studies have shown that teams that engage in mindful communication are more likely to arrive at creative solutions, as the practice encourages open dialogue, active listening, and respect for diverse perspectives (Good et al., 2016). When team members feel comfortable expressing their ideas and concerns without fear of judgment, they are more likely to contribute meaningfully to the discussion.

In personal relationships, mindful communication allows individuals to express themselves more authentically. When we communicate mindfully, we take the time to reflect on what we genuinely want to say, ensuring that our words align with our intentions. This reduces the likelihood of misunderstandings, hurt feelings, or unresolved conflicts. In romantic relationships, for example, mindful communication can help partners navigate complicated conversations about emotions, needs, or expectations with greater ease. Rather than reacting impulsively during disagreements, mindful couples listen with curiosity, validate each other's feelings, and respond with care. This approach fosters trust and emotional intimacy, deepening the connection between partners over time.

Mindful communication also includes non-verbal elements, such as body language, facial expressions, and eye contact. These non-verbal cues are as important as the words we speak, as they convey our presence and attention in the interaction. Being mindful of these aspects helps prevent miscommunication, ensuring we convey the right message with our whole presence. For example, crossing your arms during a conversation might unintentionally signal defensiveness, even if your words are neutral or positive. Similarly, avoiding eye contact can make the other person feel as though you are disinterested or disengaged. When we practice mindful communication, we become more aware of these subtle cues and can adjust our body language to match the intention behind our words.

In personal and professional contexts, mindful communication involves recognizing and acknowledging the emotions in a conversation. Emotions often color how we communicate, influencing our words' tone, pace, and intensity. When we bring mindfulness into our communication, we become attuned to our emotional state and the other person's. For instance, practicing mindfulness can help you take a step back, regulate your emotions, and communicate more calmly if you feel anxious or frustrated during a conversation. Similarly, being aware of the other person's emotions allows you to respond with greater empathy, offering validation and support.

One key aspect of mindful communication is pausing before responding. In the heat of a conversation, especially when emotions run high, it is easy to react impulsively or say something we later regret. Mindfulness encourages us to pause, take a breath, and consider our responses carefully. This pause creates a moment of reflection where we can evaluate our emotions, recognize any judgments or biases influencing our reaction, and choose a more thoughtful, constructive response. Over time, this practice helps us develop greater emotional regulation and improves the quality of our interactions.

The importance of mindful communication can also be seen in the context of conflict resolution. Whether in personal or professional relationships, conflicts are inevitable. However, how we handle those conflicts makes all the difference. Mindful communication helps de-escalate tension by fostering an atmosphere of respect and understanding. Instead of becoming defensive or shutting down during a disagreement, mindful communicators remain open to the other person's perspective and work collaboratively to find a solution. This approach resolves the immediate conflict and strengthens the relationship by building trust and mutual respect.

Furthermore, practicing mindful communication has long-term benefits for mental health and well-being. Conversations that are rushed, shallow, or filled with conflict can leave us feeling stressed, drained, and disconnected. In contrast, mindful communication enhances our connection to others, promotes empathy and compassion, and reduces the stress associated with misunderstandings or unresolved issues. By cultivating mindfulness in our conversations, we create meaningful connections and experience greater emotional satisfaction in our relationships.

Mindful communication is a powerful practice that transforms how we interact with others, whether in personal or professional settings. We can foster more profound, authentic connections by being fully present, listening without judgment, and responding intentionally. Mindful communication enhances collaboration in the workplace, promotes emotional intimacy in personal relationships, and helps us navigate conflict with grace and empathy. Ultimately, by bringing mindfulness into our conversations, we cultivate a more compassionate, understanding, and harmonious way of relating to those around us.

Barriers to Effective Communication

Effective communication is essential for building strong relationships, whether personal or professional. However, numerous barriers can hinder this process, preventing us from truly connecting with others. One of the most common barriers to effective communication is listening with the intent to reply rather than to understand genuinely. When we engage in conversations, we are often preoccupied with formulating our response while the other person is speaking. This habit stems from a desire to express our thoughts or defend our point of view, but it comes at the expense of genuinely listening. When our attention is divided this way, we miss critical conversation details, leading to misunderstandings or misinterpretations.

For example, suppose a manager is focused on preparing their rebuttal rather than listening to an employee's concerns in a workplace setting. In that case, they may miss critical feedback that could improve team dynamics. Similarly, listening to replies rather than understanding can hurt feelings and unresolved conflicts in personal relationships, as one partner may feel unheard or invalidated.

Mindfulness solves this common barrier by encouraging us to

focus entirely on the present moment and the speaker's words. Active listening, a core aspect of mindful communication, involves putting aside our internal dialogue and giving our full attention to the other person. This shift in focus allows us to listen more deeply, not just to the words being spoken but to the emotions and intentions behind them. When we listen with the goal of understanding, we create a space for more meaningful and empathetic conversations, fostering more robust connections.

Another significant barrier to effective communication is emotional reactivity. Our ability to listen and respond mindfully diminishes when we are upset, angry, or stressed. Emotional reactivity often causes us to speak impulsively, react defensively, or shut down altogether. This can escalate conflicts, leading to further misunderstandings and emotional distance between the parties involved. For example, emotional reactivity during a heated argument may cause one to lash out with hurtful words, only to regret it later. Alternatively, they may shut down completely, refusing to engage in the conversation, preventing any resolution.

Mindfulness can help mitigate emotional reactivity by teaching us to pause and observe our emotions before responding. According to Jon Kabat-Zinn (1990), mindfulness creates a "space" between stimulus and response, enabling us to choose a more thoughtful and compassionate reaction. Instead of being swept away by our emotions, mindfulness helps us stay grounded, observe our feelings without judgment, and respond in a way that aligns with our values. For example, during an argument, a mindful communicator might notice their rising anger, take a deep breath, and choose to express their feelings calmly rather than lashing out. This practice reduces the likelihood of saying something hurtful in the heat of the moment and opens the door to more productive and empathetic conversations.

Internal and external distractions are another common barrier to effective communication. In today's hyper-connected world, it is easy to become distracted by technology, such as the constant ping of notifications or the temptation to check social media during conversations. These external distractions can distract our attention from the person we are communicating with, making it challenging to stay present. Internal distractions, such as our thoughts, worries, or anxieties, can also prevent us from fully engaging in conversations. For instance, if someone is preoccupied with an upcoming deadline, they may struggle to focus on a conversation with a friend or colleague, missing important cues or failing to respond appropriately.

Mindfulness helps us recognize these distractions and gently bring our attention back to the present moment. Practicing mindfulness makes us more aware of when our mind wanders or external distractions distract us from the conversation. For example, during a meeting, a mindful communicator might notice their mind drifting to an unrelated task and gently redirect their focus to the speaker. Similarly, in a personal setting, mindfulness can help us resist the urge to check our phones during a conversation, allowing us to be fully present with the other person. Over time, this practice strengthens our ability to maintain focus and attention, leading to more meaningful and engaged interactions.

Preconceived judgments or assumptions about the other person can also cloud communication and create barriers to understanding. When we enter a conversation with preconceived ideas about what the other person will say, we are less open to genuinely hearing their perspective. These judgments can stem from past experiences, stereotypes, or biases, often leading us to interpret the other person's words through a distorted lens. For example, suppose you believe a colleague is always negative or critical. In that case, you might dismiss their feedback in a meeting, assuming they complain rather than offer constructive input. Similarly, preconceived judgments about a partner's intentions can lead to misunderstandings and resentment in personal relationships.

Mindfulness encourages us to let go of these judgments and approach each conversation with openness and curiosity. By staying present and fully engaged in the conversation, we can listen to the other person without the filter of our preconceived notions, allowing for a more accurate and compassionate understanding of their perspective. For instance, instead of assuming that a colleague is being negative, a mindful communicator might listen to their concerns with curiosity, asking questions to clarify their point of view and seeking to understand the underlying emotions behind their words. This openness creates space for more authentic and respectful communication, fostering deeper connections and reducing the potential for conflict.

Another barrier to effective communication is language and cultural differences. In an increasingly globalized world, we often interact with people from diverse cultural backgrounds, each with communication styles, values, and norms. These differences can sometimes lead to miscommunication, as what is considered polite or appropriate in one culture may be perceived differently in another. For example, in some cultures, direct eye contact is a sign of respect; in others, it may be seen as confrontational. Similarly, certain words or phrases may carry different connotations depending on the cultural context.

Mindfulness can help bridge these gaps by fostering greater cultural awareness and sensitivity. When we approach conversations mindfully, we become more attuned to the nuances of communication, including non-verbal cues, tone of voice, and cultural context. This heightened awareness allows us to navigate cross-cultural interactions with tremendous respect and understanding, reducing the likelihood of miscommunication and fostering more inclusive and harmonious relationships.

Barriers to effective communication—such as listening with the intent to reply, emotional reactivity, distractions, preconceived judgments, and cultural differences—can hinder our ability to connect with others on a deeper level. However, we can overcome these barriers by integrating mindfulness into our communication practices and fostering more meaningful, compassionate, and authentic interactions. Mindfulness helps us stay present, listen without judgment, and respond with empathy, creating the space for deeper understanding and stronger connections in personal and professional relationships.

Practicing Mindful Listening

Mindful listening is an essential practice that allows us to connect with others more deeply. Conversations often need more attention in our fast-paced world, leaving people feeling unheard or misunderstood. Mindful listening, however, involves entirely focusing on the speaker with the intent to understand, not just to reply. This practice goes beyond simply hearing words; it includes tuning into the speaker's tone of voice, body language, and emotional state. By committing to mindful listening, we create an environment of trust and respect where genuine communication can thrive.

The act of mindful listening requires being present in the moment. When someone else speaks, our minds are often preoccupied with other thoughts—formulating responses, preparing to defend our point of view, or getting distracted by unrelated concerns. This tendency to disengage from the conversation can lead to misunderstandings and shallow interactions. In contrast, mindful listening is a conscious effort to quiet our inner dialogue and focus entirely on what the other person is saying. This form of attentive listening can dramatically improve both personal and professional relationships, as it demonstrates genuine interest and empathy towards the speaker.

Active listening is a core component of mindful communication and is often described as the foundation of meaningful conversations. It involves listening attentively without interrupting or formulating a response while the other person is speaking. Research has shown that active listening leads to better communication outcomes, such as increased satisfaction, mutual understanding, and stronger relationships (Brown et al., 2007). Active listening is not just about being silent while someone speaks but also about engaging fully with what they are saying. It requires putting aside our thoughts, emotions, and distractions to focus entirely on the speaker's message. For instance, a manager who practices active listening with their employees can create a more inclusive and productive environment in a workplace setting. Employees feel valued and understood, leading to higher morale and better performance.

Active listening can deepen emotional intimacy in personal relationships by showing that we are fully present for our partners, friends, or family members. Imagine a conversation between two partners: one expresses frustration about their day, but instead of offering immediate advice or dismissing the complaint, the listener fully engages by acknowledging their partner's emotions and asking thoughtful questions. This interaction builds trust and fosters emotional support, strengthening the relationship.

One powerful way to practice mindful listening is using the "pause before response" technique. This technique encourages reflection before replying, allowing us to thoroughly absorb the speaker's message. This pause creates space for a more thoughtful and measured response, reducing the likelihood of reactive or impulsive replies. In high-stress situations, such as during arguments or disagreements, the "pause before response" technique can help de-escalate tension and foster more constructive communication. For example, instead of responding immediately to a critical remark, a mindful communicator might take a deep breath, consider the other person's perspective, and then offer a calm and respectful reply. This helps prevent conflicts from escalating and encourages more meaningful dialogue where both parties feel heard and respected.

Another helpful practice in mindful listening is non-verbal acknowledgment. While verbal communication is essential, non-verbal cues such as nodding, maintaining eye contact, or offering a smile can reinforce the speaker's sense that we are fully engaged in the conversation. Non-verbal acknowledgment shows the speaker that we are listening, even if we are not speaking, and conveys empathy and understanding. For example, during a team meeting, a manager might nod in agreement as an employee shares their thoughts, signaling that their input is being valued. In a personal conversation, maintaining eye contact while a friend shares their struggles can communicate genuine care and concern, even without saying a word.

When we listen mindfully, we are not just paying attention to the speaker's words but also attuned to their emotional state. This listening fosters empathy, allowing us to understand better and connect with the other person on a deeper level. Mindful listening helps us recognize the emotions behind the words —joy, frustration, sadness, or excitement—and respond with greater sensitivity and compassion. For instance, a colleague may express frustration over a challenging project, but mindful listening allows us to pick up on feelings of overwhelm or self-doubt. Acknowledging these emotions can offer support beyond the surface issue, strengthening the relationship and communication.

In professional environments, mindful listening is valuable for fostering collaboration and teamwork. When team members feel that their ideas and concerns are genuinely heard, they are more likely to contribute actively and work towards collective goals. This sense of psychological safety, created through mindful listening, can lead to higher levels of innovation and problem-solving within a team. Additionally, mindful leaders who practice active listening can build trust and rapport with their teams, increasing employee engagement and loyalty.

In personal relationships, mindful listening can transform how we connect with our loved ones. Being fully present and attuned to their needs shows that we value their thoughts and emotions, which can lead to deeper emotional bonds. Whether it is a partner sharing their day, a friend opening up about a challenging experience, or a family member expressing joy, mindful listening allows us to be there for them in a meaningful and supportive way.

Mindful listening is a practice that goes beyond simply hearing words; it involves being fully present, listening with the intent to understand, and responding with empathy and thoughtfulness. By incorporating techniques such as active listening, the "pause before response," and nonverbal acknowledgment, we can create more meaningful and authentic connections in our personal and professional lives. Mindful listening fosters deeper relationships, enhances collaboration, and promotes a greater sense of understanding and compassion in all areas of communication.

Techniques for Mindful Speech

Mindful speech is a powerful aspect of communication that focuses on intentionally using words to foster clarity, compassion, and understanding. Just as mindful listening helps us connect more deeply with others, mindful speech allows us to convey our thoughts and feelings in a way that promotes healthy, productive, and meaningful interactions. In an age where words are exchanged rapidly—through conversations, emails, and social media—practicing mindful speech encourages us to slow down and reflect on the impact our words can have on others.

How we speak—tone, word choice, or the underlying intent—can significantly shape how others perceive us and the quality of our relationships. Mindful speech goes beyond simply choosing words carefully; it is about speaking with purpose and awareness, ensuring that our words align with our values and have a positive impact. When we engage in mindful speech, we make a conscious effort to express ourselves in ways that are clear, compassionate, and free from unnecessary negativity. This mindful approach to speaking fosters trust, reduces misunderstandings, and enhances connection with others, whether in personal or professional settings.

A powerful tool for mindful speech is the "Three Gates" technique. This practice encourages us to pause before speaking and ask ourselves three essential questions: Is it true? Is it kind? Is it necessary? These three gates act as filters for our words, ensuring that what we are about to say is thoughtful and considerate. The first gate, "Is it true?" reminds us to speak honestly and honestly. We should avoid spreading misinformation, rumors, or making assumptions that could lead to harm or confusion. By ensuring our words are rooted in truth, we can foster trust and credibility in our relationships.

The second gate, "Is it kind?" urges us to consider the emotional impact of our words on others. Even if a statement is true, it may only be kind or helpful sometimes. Practicing kindness in our speech can promote empathy and understanding, reducing the likelihood of causing unnecessary hurt or conflict. For example, offering constructive feedback with a compassionate tone rather than harsh criticism can significantly affect how the message is received. Lastly, the third gate, "Is it necessary?" prompts us to reflect on whether the words we are about to say serve a meaningful purpose. Sometimes, the most mindful response is silence, especially when speaking may escalate a situation or add unnecessary complexity. This final filter helps us practice restraint, ensuring our speech is purposeful and aligned with the moment's needs.

Another essential technique for mindful speech is the practice of slowing down. In today's fast-paced world, we often rush through conversations, babbling and needing to fully think through what we want to convey. Slowing down our speech allows us to speak with greater intention and clarity. When we slow down, we create space for more meaningful dialogue, allowing ourselves and the listener to process what is being said. Speaking more slowly reduces the risk of misunderstandings and encourages deeper reflection and a more thoughtful exchange of ideas. For instance, during a heated discussion, slowing down your speech can help to diffuse tension, giving both parties time to think more clearly and respond calmly.

Slowing down also provides room for mindful pauses, which can be incredibly effective in communication. Introducing brief pauses before responding gives us time to process emotions, reflect on our thoughts, and choose words carefully. These pauses also allow others to feel heard and understood, as they can sense that we genuinely consider their point of view. In workplace meetings or personal conversations, these small moments of stillness can lead to more thoughtful and productive interactions, reducing the chances of reactive or impulsive responses that can escalate conflicts.

Another powerful tool for mindful speech is Non-Violent Communication (NVC), a method developed by psychologist Marshall Rosenberg in the 1960s. NVC focuses on communicating our needs and feelings in a way that avoids blame, criticism, or defensiveness. The core of NVC is expressing compassion while also being open to hearing the needs and feelings of others. NVC encourages using "I" statements rather than "you" statements, which helps to express personal feelings without making the other person feel attacked or blamed. For example, instead of saying, "You never listen to me," which may provoke defensiveness, a person practicing NVC might say, "I feel unheard when we talk, and I would like to have more meaningful conversations." This shift in language creates space for more productive, understanding-based dialogue rather than conflict or confrontation.

NVC also emphasizes the importance of empathic listening as part of mindful speech. Empathic listening involves being fully present with the speaker, not just hearing their words but also tuning into their underlying emotions and needs. This deeper level of listening enables more compassionate and effective responses. When practicing NVC, we are encouraged to identify and acknowledge the feelings and needs behind our words and those of others. By recognizing these underlying emotions and desires, we can communicate with greater understanding and connection.

For instance, in a workplace setting, using NVC can improve communication between team members, especially during moments of disagreement or stress. If an employee feels overwhelmed by their workload, instead of accusing their manager of giving too many tasks, they could say, "I feel stressed because my current workload is heavy, and I need support to manage it." This approach focuses on the employee's feelings and needs rather than casting blame, which increases the likelihood of a positive and supportive response from the manager.

In addition to the "Three Gates" technique, slowing down speech, and Non-Violent Communication, mindful speech can also include **the power of silence**. In some situations, choosing not to speak can be just as important as knowing what to say. Silence allows for reflection, both for us and for others. It creates space for understanding and can prevent words that may later be regretted. When used mindfully, silence can promote a deeper connection between people, as it shows that we are comfortable being present with one another without the need to fill every moment with words.

Lastly, mindful speech involves paying attention to our **tone of voice**. Sometimes, not what we say but how we say it has the most significant impact. A calm, respectful tone can make even tricky conversations more manageable, while an angry or impatient tone can escalate a situation. By becoming aware of our tone, we can ensure that our words align with our intention to communicate with kindness and respect.

Mindful speech is a practice that allows us to speak with purpose, clarity, and compassion. By incorporating techniques such as the "Three Gates," slowing down, Non-Violent Communication, and silence, we can enhance our ability to communicate in ways that foster understanding and connection. Whether in our personal relationships or professional environments, mindful speech can transform the way we interact with others, creating more harmonious and productive exchanges.

Real-life examples offer invaluable insights into the power of mindful communication and its ability to transform relationships—whether in personal interactions or professional settings. Through the stories of individuals who have integrated mindfulness into their communication habits, we can observe how this practice improves the quality of dialogue and nurtures trust, empathy, and emotional connection. This section will detail how mindful communication has been critical in positively reshaping work environments and intimate relationships.

One compelling case study is that of Diana, a successful business executive who initially struggled with communication within her team. Despite her leadership position, Diana found that her conversations often left her employees feeling unheard and disengaged. Her communication style involved frequent interruptions, and she was more focused on formulating her response than genuinely listening to the person speaking. This behavior created a disconnect between her and her team, leading to a lack of cohesion and trust within the workplace.

Recognizing that her communication was becoming a barrier to effective team collaboration, Diana decided to adopt mindful communication techniques. She began by practicing active listening during team meetings. Instead of interrupting or jumping to conclusions, she consciously listened fully to what each person had to say, giving her undivided attention to the speaker. Over time, this practice allowed her better to understand her team members' needs and concerns, fostering an environment of mutual respect and open dialogue.

Additionally, Diana began implementing the pause-before-response technique, which involved reflecting on what had been said before offering her reply. This brief pause allowed her to process her thoughts and signal to her employees that she valued their input. As a result, her team meetings became more productive, with employees feeling more comfortable sharing their ideas and opinions. The shift in Diana's communication approach led to more vital team unity, improved problem-solving capabilities, and a more trusting work atmosphere.

Another powerful example comes from the personal realm: a couple facing significant marriage challenges due to poor communication. Both partners, John and Emily, were experiencing frequent conflicts that stemmed from misunderstandings and reactive responses during conversations. They were stuck in a cycle of frustration, where each argument escalated without resolution, leaving both feeling unheard and disconnected.

John and Emily decided to incorporate mindful communication into their daily interactions at the recommendation of a relationship therapist. They committed to practicing several vital techniques, including the "pause before response" method, and they began using "I" statements to express their feelings. The goal was to shift the focus from blame and defensiveness to open, non-judgmental dialogue.

The pause before responding allowed John and Emily to recover from their immediate emotional reactions. Instead of interrupting or jumping to conclusions, they allowed each other to express their thoughts and emotions fully. This simple practice drastically reduced the intensity of their arguments, providing a moment of reflection that diffused tension and created an opportunity for empathy.

"I" statements also played a pivotal role in transforming their communication. Rather than saying, "You never listen to me," which often led to defensiveness, they started saying, "I feel unheard when we talk," which allowed them to communicate their emotions without assigning blame. This shift in language facilitated deeper understanding and encouraged both partners to approach each conversation more compassionately. Over time, John and Emily noticed a significant improvement in their ability to resolve conflicts, as they were now approaching disagreements with patience, mindfulness, and empathy.

Another powerful story of transformation comes from David, a healthcare worker who faced his profession's intense emotional and physical demands. Working long hours in a high-stress environment, David found that his interactions with colleagues and patients were becoming strained. He often felt overwhelmed and emotionally exhausted, leading to reactive and sometimes harsh communication. This created tension within his workplace and affected his relationships with coworkers and patients.

David enrolled in a Mindfulness-Based Stress Reduction (MBSR) program to manage his stress and improve his communication. He learned to practice mindful communication techniques through the program, including mindful listening and speech. One of the most effective tools for David was learning to incorporate body scans into his daily routine, which allowed him to become more attuned to his emotional and physical states before engaging in conversations. By recognizing when he was feeling tense or stressed, he could regulate his responses and avoid lashing out in moments of frustration.

David also began using non-violent communication (NVC) techniques to express his needs without blame or criticism. This approach helped him build stronger connections with his patients, as he could now communicate with more kindness and empathy. Instead of feeling like he had to solve every problem or respond to every emotion immediately, David became more comfortable simply listening and acknowledging the feelings of those around him. His relationships with colleagues also improved as they noticed his calmer, more grounded approach to communication.

In addition to these individual stories, mindful communication has been successfully applied in educational settings. One case involves a schoolteacher named Maria, who struggled to manage a classroom of energetic students. The students often interrupted one another, leading to chaos during class discussions and frustration on Maria's part. Maria introduced mindful communication practices to her students to address the issue, teaching them the value of mindful listening and mindful speech.

Maria implemented a classroom exercise where students would take turns speaking while others practiced mindful listening. Students could share their thoughts without interruption while their peers listened quietly and attentively. This practice improved the students' listening skills and created a more respectful and collaborative classroom environment. By teaching her students to communicate mindfully, Maria saw a significant reduction in classroom disruptions and an increase in meaningful, thoughtful discussions.

In all these cases, mindful communication was a transformative tool that enhanced personal and professional relationships. Whether in a corporate boardroom, a marriage, a healthcare setting, or a classroom, mindful communication helped individuals build deeper connections, foster trust, and navigate challenging conversations with greater ease and empathy. These stories highlight the profound impact that mindfulness can have on communication, and they serve as a reminder that with practice, we can all learn to communicate more effectively, compassionately, and mindfully.

In this chapter's next final section, pause and reflect on your communication habits and explore how you can apply mindfulness to improve daily interactions. Life's fast-paced demands often lead us into patterns of distracted listening, half-hearted conversations, and reactive responses. However, with mindful communication, we can break free from these habits and engage in more meaningful, intentional dialogue. The key is to recognize areas that need improvement and take deliberate steps to transform them.

Step 1: Reflect On Your Communication Habits

Reflection is a vital tool in this process. Take a moment to consider your typical communication style. Are there times when you find yourself distracted during conversations? Do you tend to interrupt others or start forming your response before the other person has finished speaking? Recognizing these patterns helps you identify barriers to genuine connection. Once you identify areas for improvement, you can use mindfulness to cultivate awareness, presence, and compassion in communication.

To guide this reflection, use this journaling prompt: *"Think of a recent conversation where you were not fully present. How might mindfulness have changed that interaction?"* Review a past conversation and consider how your distracted or reactive tendencies may have influenced the outcome. Reflect on whether mindful listening could have made the conversation more meaningful or productive. Could pausing before responding have fostered deeper understanding or connection? This journaling exercise helps you bridge the gap between theory and real-life application, allowing you to reflect on your growth and challenges consciously.

Step 2: Observe Your Emotional Responses In Conversations

Pay attention to how you respond during challenging or emotionally charged conversations. Do you become defensive or reactive? Are there moments when emotions cloud your judgment, leading to misunderstandings or conflict? By observing your emotional responses, you can identify opportunities for mindfulness to create space between your emotions and reactions. Practicing mindful awareness in these moments enables you to respond thoughtfully and compassionately, reducing the chances of miscommunication and conflict.

Step 3: Practice Mindful Listening

Mindful listening is a powerful tool to deepen your communication skills. The next time you engage in a conversation—whether at work, with family, or socially—commit to practicing deep listening. Focus entirely on the speaker, consciously tune out distractions, and resist the urge to interrupt or mentally prepare a response. Instead, listen with an open mind and heart, paying attention to the words and the speaker's tone, body language, and emotions.

Mindful listening requires you to be fully present in the moment, which is the cornerstone of mindful communication. By focusing on the speaker, you cultivate empathy and understanding beyond surface-level conversation. This approach can be especially beneficial in relationships with frequent miscommunication or emotional dynamics that make conversations more challenging.

Step 4: Reflect And Journal About Your Listening Practice

After practicing mindful listening, take some time to journal about your experience. How did mindfulness impact the quality of the conversation? Did you notice a change in your emotional response? Were you able to resist the urge to interrupt or react impulsively? This reflective practice helps reinforce the benefits of mindful communication, making it a regular part of your communication style.

Step 5: Apply Mindful Communication To Different Areas Of Your Life

Consider how mindfulness can enhance communication in various aspects of your life. For example:

- Workplace Interactions: How can mindful communication improve colleague relationships, foster teamwork, and create a more positive work environment? Mindfulness can help you remain calm and centered, allowing for more transparent, more thoughtful dialogue.
- Personal Relationships: How can mindful communication strengthen bonds with romantic

partners, friends, or family? Mindful listening and speech foster trust, reduce conflict and deepen emotional connections. You can improve communication in personal interactions by expressing needs and feelings clearly while understanding others' perspectives.

Step 6: Use Scenarios To Explore Mindfulness In Communication

In a final journaling exercise, reflect on how mindfulness can shape communication in specific contexts:

- How might it help you navigate difficult conversations with a partner or resolve conflicts with a friend?
- How could it enhance your leadership skills at work or improve collaboration with colleagues?

Exploring these scenarios through mindfulness helps you gain deeper insights into the practical applications of mindful communication in everyday situations.

Step 7: Cultivate Long-Term Changes

Over time, mindful communication can significantly improve how you relate to others. As you become more present, compassionate, and intentional in your conversations, you will likely see positive changes in the quality of your relationships. Misunderstandings will decrease, emotional connections will strengthen, and conflict will be easier to manage.

Ultimately, mindful communication is about improving relationships and cultivating inner peace and emotional resilience. By making mindfulness a daily habit—whether through listening, speaking, or reflection—you can break the cycle of distracted, reactive communication and foster a state of presence and balance. This practice will enable you to navigate the complexities of human interaction with grace, empathy, and understanding while enhancing your emotional awareness, mental clarity, and capacity for meaningful conversations.

References

- Brown, K. W., Ryan, R. M., & Creswell, J. D. (2007). Mindfulness: Theoretical foundations and evidence for its salutary effects. *Psychological Inquiry, 18*(4), 211-237.
- Good, D. J., Lyddy, C. J., Glomb, T. M., Bono, J. E., Brown, K. W., Duffy, M. K., & Lazar, S. W. (2016). Contemplating mindfulness at work: An integrative review. *Journal of Management, 42*(1), 114-142.
- Kabat-Zinn, J. (1990). *Whole Catastrophe Living: Using the Wisdom of Your Body and Mind to Face Stress, Pain, and Illness.* Delacorte Press.
- Rosenberg, M. B. (2003). *Nonviolent Communication: A Language of Life.* PuddleDancer Press.
- Siegel, D. J. (2010). *The Mindful Brain: Reflection and Attunement in the Cultivation of Well-being.* W.W. Norton & Company.

CHAPTER 9: THE MINDFUL BODY

The Connection Between Body and Mind

The mind and body are deeply interconnected, functioning in unison to influence and shape our well-being. While many mindfulness practices focus primarily on mental awareness—such as observing thoughts, emotions, or breathing—mindfulness of the body offers a gateway to even more profound levels of self-awareness. The body serves as a direct reflection of our mental and emotional states. Every thought or emotion we experience manifests in the body, whether it is a surge of energy when we are excited or a knot in the stomach when we are anxious. We can develop greater emotional resilience, physical health, and a more integrated approach to mindfulness by tuning into the body's signals- sensations, posture, and movement.

In our fast-paced world, becoming disconnected from our bodies is easy. Many of us spend long hours seated at desks, moving mechanically through our daily routines, often ignoring the subtle cues our bodies are giving us. These cues can be signals of tension, stress, fatigue, or even joy, but we may overlook them due to distractions or a lack of awareness. Mindful body awareness helps bridge the gap between how we feel emotionally and physically experience those emotions. It allows us to reconnect with our bodies, to notice when and where tension builds, and to explore how our physical states influence our emotional well-being. Becoming more attuned to our bodily sensations creates a direct path to understanding and regulating our emotions more effectively.

Mindful body awareness can take many different forms. For example, when stressed, we might notice tension in our shoulders, a clenched jaw, or shallow breathing. These physical sensations often go unnoticed, but we can address the underlying emotional triggers when we become aware. Similarly, we can become mindful of how our posture affects our emotional states. Studies have shown that standing or sitting up straight with an open posture can help boost confidence and elevate mood. At the same time, slouching can trigger or exacerbate negative emotions like sadness or lethargy. By making minor adjustments in our body's position or alignment, we can influence our mental state, shifting from anxiety or frustration to calmness and centeredness.

By incorporating mindfulness into the body's physical sensations, people can reduce stress, prevent burnout, and improve concentration. Mindful practices like body scanning and mindful movement are practical tools for achieving this. Body scanning involves slowly and intentionally bringing awareness to different parts of the body, noticing sensations without judgment, and releasing any tension that may be present. This practice helps individuals become more in tune with their body's needs and promotes relaxation and healing. Mindful movement, whether through yoga, Tai Chi, or simply walking, encourages a greater connection between the body and the mind. Moving with awareness, focusing on each step, stretch, or breath, brings the mind into the present moment and enhances emotional regulation.

A growing body of research supports the profound benefits of mindful body awareness on emotional and physical well-being. A study published in the *Journal of Cognitive Enhancement* found that participants who practiced mindfulness techniques, such as body scanning and mindful movement, experienced significant improvements in focus, reduced anxiety levels, and enhanced overall well-being (Zeidan et al., 2010). These findings highlight the critical role that the body plays in shaping mental health and emphasize the importance of adopting a holistic approach to mindfulness. When we listen to and respond to our body's signals, we become more aware of how our physical and mental states interact, allowing us to cultivate greater self-awareness and emotional balance.

The importance of mindful body awareness extends beyond just stress management. It can also be a powerful tool for preventing chronic stress-related illnesses and improving overall physical health. For example, chronic stress often leads to physical symptoms such as headaches, muscle tension, digestive issues, and sleep disturbances. By regularly tuning into the body's sensations, individuals can catch these early signs of stress before they escalate into more severe health problems. Furthermore, mindful body awareness can enhance physical performance in exercise, daily activities, or even professional settings. When individuals are fully present in their bodies, they become more attuned to their movements, energy levels, and limits, allowing for greater efficiency and ease in their actions.

Understanding the body's role in shaping mental health creates a more holistic approach to mindfulness that encompasses mental and physical awareness. Acknowledging the body as an integral part of our emotional and cognitive processes opens the door to more profound healing and personal growth. By practicing mindfulness of the body, we develop a greater sense of groundedness, emotional resilience, and overall well-being. This practice encourages us to live in harmony with our physical selves, fostering a sense of balance that can carry over into all aspects of our lives. Whether managing daily stressors or seeking to improve our physical and emotional health, mindful body awareness provides the foundation for a more integrated, peaceful, and fulfilling life.

Mindfulness and Physical Health

The connection between mindfulness and physical health is increasingly well-documented in scientific literature, and it is becoming more widely recognized as a crucial component of overall well-being. Numerous studies highlight mindfulness practices' profound impact on various physical health outcomes. Incorporating mindfulness into daily life leads to improvements such as lowered blood pressure, reduced chronic pain, enhanced immune function, and better sleep quality (Creswell, 2017). These benefits are primarily attributed to mindfulness's ability to regulate the body's stress response, critical in developing and progressing many health conditions.

Stress is one of the significant contributors to poor physical health, particularly in today's fast-paced, high-pressure world. When we encounter stress, our bodies release cortisol and adrenaline, two essential hormones that prepare us for "fight or flight" responses. While these hormones are beneficial in short-term situations, they help us respond to immediate threats, such as chronic stress and prolonged exposure to them, which can damage our health. Over time, high levels of cortisol can weaken the immune system, increase blood pressure, and heighten the risk of developing heart disease, digestive problems, and other stress-related illnesses. Mindfulness helps counteract these effects by encouraging relaxation and engaging the parasympathetic nervous system (PNS)—the "rest and digest" system that allows the body to recover, repair, and maintain equilibrium.

By practicing mindfulness, individuals learn to observe their thoughts and bodily sensations without judgment, which helps them recognize and manage stress before it escalates into a full-blown health crisis. For instance, mindful awareness can help identify early signs of stress, such as tight muscles or shallow breathing, instead of allowing worries to spiral into physical tension. Mindful practices like deep breathing, progressive muscle relaxation, and body scanning allow individuals to release tension and restore balance to their body's systems. Studies have shown that regular mindfulness practice is associated with lower levels of inflammatory markers in the body, which are linked to chronic diseases like heart disease, diabetes, and arthritis (Davidson & McEwen, 2012). The body's ability to regulate inflammation improves significantly when mindfulness is incorporated into daily routines, offering a protective buffer against stress-induced illnesses.

Incorporating mindfulness into physical activities such as walking, stretching, or yoga can enhance these health benefits. Mindful movement practices like yoga and Tai Chi combine the principles of mindfulness with physical exercise, encouraging participants to remain present and attentive to their bodies during each movement. This mindful awareness of movement helps strengthen the mind-body connection, allowing individuals to tune into their physical sensations, improve posture, and maintain balance. Research has consistently shown that people who engage in mindful movement experience improved cardiovascular health, greater flexibility, and increased strength (Morone et al., 2008). In addition to physical fitness, these practices promote relaxation, helping alleviate mental and physical tension.

For example, a study published in *The American Journal of Medicine* found that participants who practiced mindful movement exercises, such as yoga and Tai Chi, experienced significant reductions in chronic pain and stress levels (Morone et al., 2008). Many participants reported improved mobility, physical function, and greater emotional well-being. Individuals can cultivate a more profound sense of presence and relaxation by focusing on each movement and synchronizing it with the breath. These practices are particularly beneficial for people dealing with chronic pain conditions, as mindful movement provides a gentle yet effective way to move the body without exacerbating pain symptoms.

Mindfulness-based interventions, such as Mindfulness-Based Stress Reduction (MBSR), have also been shown to alleviate symptoms of a wide range of chronic illnesses, including rheumatoid arthritis, fibromyalgia, irritable bowel syndrome (IBS), and chronic fatigue syndrome. Through meditation, body awareness, and mindful movement, individuals approach their physical symptoms with curiosity and compassion rather than resistance or frustration (Kabat-Zinn, 1990). This shift in perspective helps reduce the emotional toll of chronic illness and enhances the body's capacity to heal.

For instance, individuals with chronic pain often experience a cycle of pain, stress, and tension, where stress worsens pain, and the pain, in turn, increases stress levels. Mindfulness offers a way to interrupt this cycle by encouraging individuals to bring attention to the physical sensations in their bodies without attaching negative judgments or fears to them. They can develop a greater tolerance for discomfort and reduce the emotional reactivity accompanying chronic pain. A growing body of research supports the use of MBSR in reducing not only physical pain but also the emotional distress associated with chronic conditions (Baer, 2006). Mindfulness teaches individuals to be present with their pain, observe it from a non-judgmental perspective, and let go of the mental narratives that often make the experience of pain worse.

The impact of mindfulness on physical health extends beyond managing chronic conditions. It can also improve immune function, lower the risk of developing stress-related illnesses, and enhance overall quality of life. Studies have shown that individuals who practice mindfulness regularly have a more robust immune response to illness and infection (Creswell, 2017). By engaging the parasympathetic nervous system, mindfulness promotes healing, strengthens the body's natural defenses, and reduces the wear and tear that chronic stress can have on the immune system. Additionally, mindfulness practices such as mindful eating can promote healthier dietary habits, improve digestion and weight management, and reduce inflammation. By paying close attention to hunger and fullness cues, individuals can make more informed, mindful choices about what and how much to eat, resulting in better long-term health outcomes.

Techniques for Mindful Movement

The mindful movement goes beyond the boundaries of traditional exercise. It is a holistic approach to physical activity that emphasizes cultivating awareness of the body's sensations, rhythm, and movements in the present moment. While traditional exercises may focus primarily on physical fitness, mindful movement invites a deeper connection between the body and mind, fostering physical strength, mental clarity, and emotional well-being. Whether walking, stretching, or engaging in structured practices like yoga or tai chi, mindful movement offers a powerful way for individuals to reconnect with their physical selves and cultivate a sense of peace and balance in their daily lives.

One of the most straightforward and accessible forms of mindful movement is mindful walking. Unlike ordinary walking, which is often rushed and performed mindlessly to reach a destination, mindful walking is a meditative practice in which individuals focus intently on each step, becoming fully present in walking. Practitioners are encouraged to bring their awareness to the sensation of their feet touching the ground, the shifting weight in their legs, the rhythm of their steps, and the feeling of their bodies moving through space. Mindful walking transforms an everyday activity into a profoundly grounding practice by focusing on these sensations. Research has shown that mindful walking can reduce stress, lower blood pressure, alleviate anxiety, and improve overall mood (Wong et al., 2019). It provides an opportunity to step out of the mental chatter and embrace the simplicity and rhythm of each step, offering both physical and emotional benefits.

Mindful walking can be practiced anywhere—in a park, city street, or indoors. The key is to slow down, pay attention to each movement, and remain present in the moment. For those who find it challenging to sit still during traditional seated meditation, mindful walking provides an excellent alternative that allows them to maintain a state of mindfulness while staying physically active. Additionally, mindful walking encourages individuals to appreciate their surroundings, heightening awareness of the environment's sights, sounds, and smells, which can deepen their connection to nature and the world around them.

Yoga is another powerful tool for cultivating mindful movement, and its benefits extend far beyond physical fitness. While many people view yoga as a form of exercise that increases flexibility and strength, the practice of yoga is rooted in mindfulness and meditation. In a typical yoga session, practitioners are encouraged to focus on their breath, align their body with each pose, and bring their awareness to the physical sensations that arise during the practice. The emphasis on deep breathing and mindful awareness helps practitioners remain present in each moment, fostering a sense of inner calm and reducing the mental distractions that often lead to stress and anxiety. Yoga's integration of mindful awareness with physical movement creates a holistic practice that benefits both the body and mind.

Research supports the mental health benefits of yoga, with numerous studies demonstrating its effectiveness in reducing symptoms of stress, anxiety, and depression. According to a study published in *The Journal of Behavioral Medicine*, regularly practicing yoga reports lower levels of perceived stress, better mood regulation, and enhanced emotional well-being (Smith et al., 2011). The physical postures (asanas) in yoga help build strength, flexibility, and balance, while the meditative aspects of the practice encourage mindfulness, self-compassion, and mental clarity. Yoga practitioners learn to listen to their bodies, respect their limitations, and cultivate a sense of acceptance and non-judgment, further promoting emotional resilience and mental peace.

In addition to its mental health benefits, yoga has been shown to improve cardiovascular health, enhance lung function, and reduce chronic pain in individuals with various health conditions. Yoga calms the nervous system, activating the parasympathetic nervous system (PNS) and promoting relaxation. This physiological response reduces stress hormones like cortisol, improves digestion, boosts immune function, and enhances sleep quality. Combining mindful awareness with physical movement makes yoga a powerful tool for improving overall well-being and balancing body and mind.

Tai chi is another form of mindful movement that has gained recognition for its mental and physical benefits. Often described as "meditation in motion," tai chi consists of slow, deliberate movements synchronized with deep breathing. Practitioners flow through a series of graceful postures, maintaining a sense of relaxation, balance, and mindfulness throughout the practice. Unlike more vigorous forms of exercise, tai chi is gentle on the body, making it accessible to people of all ages and fitness levels. Despite its gentle nature, tai chi offers many physical and mental health benefits, particularly for older adults and individuals with limited mobility.

A study published in *The New England Journal of Medicine* found that practicing tai chi significantly improved balance and reduced the risk of falls in older adults (Wolf et al., 1996).

This is particularly important because falls are a leading cause of injury and disability among the elderly. The mindful tai chi movements improve physical balance and coordination and enhance flexibility, muscle strength, and cardiovascular health. Additionally, tai chi's emphasis on deep, mindful breathing helps calm the mind, reduce anxiety, and promote emotional stability. Like yoga, tai chi combines mindfulness with physical movement, creating a practice that fosters mental clarity and physical vitality.

Mindful movement practices like walking, yoga, and tai chi offer a bridge between physical and mental well-being. Individuals can develop a greater connection between their physical self and their mental state by cultivating awareness of the body's sensations, movements, and rhythms. These practices improve physical health—such as cardiovascular fitness, flexibility, and strength—and promote relaxation, reduce stress, and enhance emotional resilience. For those looking to incorporate mindfulness into their lives to benefit their physical health, mindful movement provides an accessible and practical approach to achieving holistic well-being.

Whether practiced through mindful walking in nature, engaging in a yoga class, or flowing through the gentle movements of tai chi, mindful movement offers many benefits that nourish both body and mind. As individuals learn to move with awareness, they cultivate a deeper understanding of their physical sensations and emotional states, leading to greater self-awareness, inner peace, and improved health outcomes. By staying present in each movement and aligning the mind with the body, mindful movement becomes a powerful tool for transforming health, well-being, and overall quality of life.

Body Scans and Mindful Awareness

The body scan is one of the most well-known mindfulness practices, designed to increase awareness of physical sensations in the body. It is a foundational practice in many mindfulness-based programs, including Mindfulness-Based Stress Reduction (MBSR), because it allows individuals to cultivate a deeper connection between their body and mind. In a body scan, the practitioner systematically focuses on different body parts, starting from the toes and moving upward toward the head. This slow and intentional process of directing attention can increase awareness of tension, discomfort, or areas of ease and relaxation throughout the body. Unlike other meditation techniques focusing solely on the breath or thoughts, body scans help bring attention to physical sensations, creating a stronger sense of embodiment and presence in the moment.

One of the significant benefits of the body scan is its ability to help individuals manage stress and anxiety by developing a greater awareness of how emotions manifest physically. When stress accumulates, it often shows up in specific areas of the body, such as tightness in the neck and shoulders, clenching in the jaw, or tension in the lower back. By practicing body scans regularly, individuals learn to recognize these early signs of stress in their bodies and address them before they become overwhelming. Research supports the effectiveness of body scans in reducing stress. A study published in the journal *Mindfulness* found that individuals who regularly practiced body scans reported significant reductions in stress levels and an improved ability to manage emotional responses to stressful situations (Grossman et al., 2004).

In addition to managing stress, body scans are particularly beneficial for those who struggle with chronic pain or discomfort. Chronic pain can be an emotionally draining experience, often leading to frustration, anger, or feelings of helplessness. Through mindful body scans, individuals can learn to observe their pain with curiosity rather than judgment. Instead of becoming overwhelmed by the intensity of the pain, they can explore how the sensations shift and change over time.

This shift in perspective can lead to greater emotional resilience and an enhanced ability to cope with pain. Studies have shown that individuals who practice body scans regularly report lower pain levels but also experience improvements in their overall quality of life and emotional well-being (Kabat-Zinn, 1990). This practice helps cultivate a sense of acceptance and self-compassion, even in the face of physical challenges.

Beyond relieving stress and pain, body scans also contribute to a broader sense of self-awareness and mindfulness. By paying close attention to the body's sensations without judgment, individuals better understand how their thoughts, emotions, and physical sensations are interconnected. This heightened awareness can lead to more mindful choices in daily life, such as taking breaks when needed, practicing self-care, or recognizing emotional triggers before they escalate. The body scan teaches us to tune in to our body's signals, which can often serve as early indicators of our emotional state. For example, a racing heart or shallow breathing might signal anxiety, while a clenched jaw might indicate frustration. By learning to identify these physical signs, individuals can take steps to address their emotional needs more effectively.

To practice a body scan, find a quiet space to lie down or sit comfortably. The body scan can be done in any position, though lying down is often recommended for beginners as it allows for complete relaxation. Begin by closing your eyes and focusing on your breath. Take a few deep breaths to center yourself in the present moment. As you breathe in and out, start to bring your awareness to your feet. Notice any sensations in your feet —whether warm or cold, tension or relaxation or perhaps even tingling or numbness. Observe these sensations without trying to change or fix them. After spending a few moments focusing on your feet, slowly direct your attention upward to your ankles, calves, and knees, observing the sensations in each area as you move along.

Continue this process as you work your way up the body. Focus on your thighs, hips, lower back, stomach, chest, and shoulders, exploring each area with curiosity and non-judgment. Notice any tension, tightness, or discomfort, and acknowledge its presence without resisting it. If your mind begins to wander, gently bring your attention back to the part of the body you were focusing on. When you reach your neck and head, pay attention to any tension in the jaw, temples, or scalp. Many people unconsciously carry stress in these areas, and simply becoming aware of it can lead to relaxation.

The body scan practice typically lasts between 15 and 25 minutes, depending on how much time you spend focusing on each body part. By the end of the practice, you may notice a more profound sense of relaxation, presence, and connection with your body. Some practitioners report feeling more grounded and centered, while others experience a release of tension they had not realized they were carrying. Body scans are often used to wind down before bed, as they can help release the day's accumulated stress and prepare the mind and body for restful sleep.

The body scan is a versatile and accessible mindfulness practice that can benefit anyone looking to improve their physical and mental well-being. Whether used to manage stress, relieve pain, or become more present daily, the body scan fosters a greater awareness and connection with the self. Regular body scans into your routine can cultivate a deeper relationship with your body and enhance your overall mindfulness practice.

Real-life examples can powerfully illustrate the transformative effects of mindful movement and body awareness on physical and mental well-being. These stories offer insights into how regular mindfulness practices can improve health, reduce chronic pain, and foster greater awareness of the body's movements, ultimately leading to an improved quality of life.

Whether addressing chronic conditions, improving mobility, or enhancing emotional resilience, mindful movement can profoundly affect people's lives.

Take the story of Jane, a 45-year-old office worker who struggled with chronic back pain for over a decade. Her job required her to sit at a desk for long hours, leading to poor posture and increased tension in her lower back. Over the years, Jane sought various treatments—physical therapy, pain medications, and even cortisone injections—but nothing provided long-term relief. After attending a mindfulness workshop, Jane was introduced to mindful walking and yoga practices. Initially skeptical about how these gentle practices could help, she decided to try them.

Over time, Jane began to incorporate mindful walking into her daily routine, paying close attention to how she placed her feet on the ground, her spine's alignment, and her hips' movement as she walked. In addition, she started practicing yoga three times a week, focusing on slow, controlled movements and deep breathing. Within a few months, Jane noticed a significant reduction in her back pain. By bringing mindful awareness to her posture and movement patterns, she became aware of how she had been holding tension in her body—particularly her shoulders and lower back. The mindful movement allowed her to release that tension and move more fluidly throughout the day. In addition to reducing her pain, Jane experienced improvements in her flexibility, mood, and energy levels. She found that practicing mindful movement also helped reduce her stress, which had been contributing to her physical discomfort.

Another compelling story comes from Mark, a 60-year-old retiree who suffered a fall that left him with balance issues and a deep sense of insecurity about his physical abilities. After his fall, Mark became afraid of walking long distances or climbing stairs, fearing that he might fall again. His physical therapist recommended tai chi, a slow-moving form of martial arts often called "meditation in motion." At first, Mark was hesitant—he did not think he had the patience or coordination for such a practice. However, after just a few sessions, Mark noticed subtle improvements in his balance and posture.

Tai chi required Mark to slow down and focus on the deliberate movements of his body. He learned to coordinate his breath with his movements, becoming more aware of how his feet, legs, and arms harmonized. Though the practice seemed simple, it required deep concentration and focus. Over time, Mark found that tai chi helped him regain his balance and confidence. Mark became more active and independent, no longer afraid of falling, allowing him to resume gardening and hiking activities he once enjoyed. Tai chi not only improved his physical coordination but also reduced his anxiety, helping him feel more at ease in his body.

A third case study involves Elena, a 38-year-old mother of two who had been struggling with high levels of stress and tension headaches for years. Juggling a full-time job with the demands of raising children, Elena often felt overwhelmed. Her headaches would come on suddenly, particularly at the end of a long workday, and nothing seemed to help alleviate the pain. After hearing about the benefits of mindfulness from a friend, Elena decided to try a body scan meditation. She found it challenging to stay focused the first few times she practiced, as her mind kept wandering to her to-do list. However, she persisted, and after a few weeks, she became more attuned to her body's physical sensations.

During one body scan practice, Elena realized that she had been unconsciously clenching her jaw throughout the day—a habit that was contributing to her tension headaches. She could catch herself in the act and consciously relax her jaw by becoming aware. Over time, her headaches became less frequent, and when they did occur, she could use mindfulness techniques like deep breathing and progressive muscle relaxation to reduce their intensity. Elena also found that body scan meditations helped her unwind before bed, improving her sleep quality and leaving her feeling more refreshed in the mornings.

These stories demonstrate how mindfulness can be applied to physical health, improving the mind and body. Reducing chronic pain, improving balance, alleviating stress, or simply becoming more attuned to physical sensations, mindful movement, and body awareness can significantly improve quality of life. These practices are accessible to individuals of all ages and abilities, offering a gentle yet powerful way to enhance physical health, emotional resilience, and mental clarity.

Incorporating mindful movement into daily routines—whether through yoga, tai chi, mindful walking, or body scan meditations—can foster a deeper connection to the body and help individuals move through the world with greater awareness and ease. For those living with chronic pain or health challenges, mindfulness provides a way to manage symptoms and cultivate a sense of empowerment over their physical well-being. As these case studies illustrate, the benefits of mindful movement extend beyond the physical body, contributing to a more balanced, peaceful, and fulfilling life.

Incorporating mindful movement into your daily routine does not have to be a monumental task or require significant time commitments. Even a few minutes each day can improve mental clarity, emotional balance, and physical well-being. Whether through mindful walking, stretching, or body scan meditations, these practices are accessible to everyone and can be seamlessly integrated into everyday life. The key is consistency and bringing awareness to the present moment, especially as you connect with your body.

One of the first steps in practicing mindful movement is to reflect on how often you check in with your body throughout the day. Many of us become so absorbed in our daily responsibilities—work, family, errands—that we lose touch with our bodies' signals. A helpful journaling prompt to begin this exploration is: "How often do you check in with your body throughout the day? What physical sensations do you notice when you are stressed or overwhelmed?" This question can help you raise awareness about your current relationship with your body, and it may reveal patterns you were not previously conscious of, such as tension in your shoulders, shallow breathing, or clenching your jaw when you are stressed.

As you become more aware of these physical cues, it is essential to create space for mindful movement practices that help release the tension and stress accumulated in the body. Integrating mindful walking into your daily routine is a simple way to start. Set aside just 10 minutes each day to walk mindfully. During this time, shift your focus away from the destination and onto the walking experience. Pay close attention to how your feet connect with the ground, the rhythmic movement of your legs, and the gentle rise and fall of your breath. Notice how your body feels in motion and whether any areas feel tight, relaxed, or energized. This practice is not about speed or distance but rather about being fully present in the movement of your body.

Practicing mindful walking offers a much-needed mental break from the day's demands. Many people report feeling more grounded and centered after just a few minutes of mindful walking, as it provides an opportunity to reconnect with their bodies gently and non-judgmentally. After your walk, take a moment to reflect on how you feel physically and emotionally. You can journal about the experience, noting any shifts in mood or body sensations. This reflection can deepen your understanding of how your body responds to mindful movement and how it affects your overall well-being.

In addition to mindful walking, another highly effective practice is body scan meditation. The body scan is particularly beneficial for those struggling with sleep, tension, or stress, as it encourages you to release physical and emotional tension from your body systematically. To begin a body scan, find a quiet space to lie down comfortably—your bed, a yoga mat, or even a couch. Close your eyes and take a few deep breaths, allowing your body to relax. Start by focusing on your toes, noticing sensations like warmth, tingling, or tension. Gradually move your attention upward, focusing on each part of your body, from your feet to your legs, torso, arms, and head.

As you conduct the body scan, pay attention to areas where you feel discomfort or tightness, but try not to judge or change these sensations. Instead, observe them with curiosity. If you encounter areas of tension, take a deep breath and imagine that with each exhale, you are releasing some of the tension. When you reach the top of your head, you may feel more at ease and relaxed, with a heightened awareness of your body. This practice is beneficial before bed, as it can help calm the nervous system and promote more profound, more restful sleep. For those who find it difficult to "turn off" their minds at night, the body scan provides a structured way to shift attention away from racing thoughts and toward the sensations in the body, encouraging relaxation.

One of the long-term benefits of regularly practicing mindful movement is the increased connection between the mind and body. When we check in with our bodies throughout the day, we become more attuned to the subtle signals that can indicate stress, discomfort, or fatigue before they escalate into more severe issues. This awareness allows us to intervene early, whether by taking a few deep breaths, stepping away from a stressful situation, or stretching to relieve tension. Over time, these small interventions can have a cumulative effect, helping to reduce chronic stress, prevent burnout, and improve overall emotional regulation.

Mindful movement can also be a powerful tool for enhancing self-compassion. In a world where we are often focused on productivity and achievement, we may neglect the basic needs of our bodies or push ourselves to the point of exhaustion. By practicing mindful movement, we learn to honor our bodies' limits and respond with care and compassion. Whether taking a mindful walk during a break from work or doing a few stretches to release tension, these practices remind us that self-care is not a luxury but a necessity for maintaining balance and well-being.

Another practice that can complement mindful movement is mindful breathing. As you go about your day, pause and focus on your breath. Notice the sensation of the air entering and leaving your body and allow your breath to anchor you in the present moment. Mindful breathing can be done anytime, anywhere—whether sitting at your desk, waiting in line, or preparing to start a new task. Incorporating mindful breathing into your routine creates more opportunities to reconnect with your body and bring awareness to how you feel physically and emotionally.

Ultimately, making mindful movement a regular part of your daily routine can profoundly change how you experience and respond to life. The more you practice, the more you will notice improvements in your physical health, mental clarity, and emotional resilience. Each small step—whether a mindful walk, a body scan, or simply pausing to check in with your breath—brings you closer to a state of balance where the mind and body work in harmony. Over time, this practice becomes a way of life, guiding you toward greater well-being, inner peace, and a deeper connection with yourself.

Mindful movement is not just about physical exercise but about developing a relationship with your body grounded in awareness, compassion, and presence. Committing to even a few minutes of mindful movement each day can cultivate a deeper connection between your mind and body, enhancing both your physical and mental health. Whether through walking, stretching, body scans, or mindful breathing, these simple yet powerful practices offer a pathway to greater well-being and a more fulfilling, balanced life.

References:

- Creswell, J. D. (2017). Mindfulness interventions. *Annual Review of Psychology, 68,* 491-516.
- Grossman, P., Niemann, L., Schmidt, S., & Walach, H. (2004). Mindfulness-based stress reduction and health benefits: A meta-analysis. *Journal of Psychosomatic Research, 57*(1), 35-43.
- Kabat-Zinn, J. (1990). *Whole Catastrophe Living: Using the Wisdom of Your Body and Mind to Face Stress, Pain, and Illness.* Delta Trade Paperbacks.
- Morone, N. E., Greco, C. M., & Weiner, D. K. (2008). Mindfulness meditation for treating chronic low back pain in older adults: A randomized controlled pilot study. *Pain, 134*(3), 310-319.
- Smith, B., et al. (2011). The effect of mindfulness-based yoga on the mental health of students. *Journal of Behavioral Medicine, 34*(6), 576–584.
- Wong, S. Y. S., et al. (2019). The effects of mindfulness-based stress reduction program on quality of life in adults with cardiovascular disease. *Journal of Behavioral Medicine, 42*(3), 518-528.
- Zeidan, F., et al. (2010). Mindfulness meditation improves cognition: Evidence of brief mental training. *Consciousness and Cognition, 19*(2), 597-605.

CHAPTER 10: COMPASSION AND SELF-COMPASSION

The Power of Compassion

Compassion is among the most potent forces in human relationships and personal well-being. It is the ability to recognize the suffering of others and the desire to alleviate that suffering, but it extends beyond outward expressions of kindness. In the context of mindfulness, compassion is a practice that allows individuals to offer kindness, understanding, and empathy to others and themselves. Compassion is the foundation of many mindfulness practices, fostering a deep sense of connection, care, and understanding. The Dalai Lama once said, "Compassion is the wish to see others free from suffering" (Dalai Lama, 2005), highlighting compassion's essential role in cultivating meaningful and positive interpersonal connections. It is a fundamental human quality that can potentially transform individual relationships and entire communities.

The power of compassion is magnified when it is integrated with mindfulness. Mindfulness allows individuals to be fully present in each moment, aware of their thoughts, emotions, and experiences without judgment. This heightened awareness creates a fertile ground for compassion to grow as individuals become more attuned to the needs, struggles, and emotions of those around them. When we are present and aware, we can see suffering more clearly and respond with empathy and care. Compassion in this form is not merely a reactive feeling but a mindful, intentional act of kindness and understanding. It allows us to listen more deeply, respond more thoughtfully, and connect more authentically with others, fostering more robust and harmonious relationships.

Scientific research supports that compassion, mainly cultivated through mindfulness practices, has profound mental and emotional health benefits. Studies have shown that practicing compassion improves relationships, decreases conflict, and increases emotional resilience (Gilbert, 2009). For example, a study conducted by Jazaieri et al. in 2013 found that participants who underwent mindfulness-based compassion training experienced significant increases in feelings of compassion for others and themselves. In addition, they reported lower levels of stress, anxiety, and depression. This research highlights that compassion is not just a passive emotion but an active practice that can improve mental health and overall well-being.

In the broader context of interpersonal relationships, compassion is a bridge that fosters understanding and reduces the likelihood of conflict. When individuals approach others with compassion, they are more likely to engage in constructive communication, demonstrate patience, and show empathy in difficult situations. Compassion also allows people to see beyond the surface-level behavior of others, recognizing that pain or suffering often lies beneath anger, frustration, or defensiveness. By responding with compassion rather than judgment or criticism, individuals can help diffuse conflict and create space for healing and resolution. This is particularly important in professional environments, where stress and high expectations often lead to misunderstandings and tension. Compassionate leadership, for instance, has been shown to improve team dynamics, increase productivity, and promote a more positive work culture.

However, compassion is not solely an outward-facing practice. It also involves self-compassion, extending the same kindness, understanding, and empathy to oneself that one would offer to a close friend or loved one. Self-compassion is essential in today's fast-paced and often demanding world, where many individuals are harshly self-critical and hold themselves to impossible standards of perfection. When we practice self-compassion, we acknowledge that it is okay to make mistakes, to feel overwhelmed, or to struggle, just as it is okay for others to do so. Instead of berating ourselves for our perceived shortcomings, we offer kindness, understanding, and forgiveness. This practice of self-compassion can lead to greater emotional resilience, as individuals can better navigate life's challenges without becoming overwhelmed by self-doubt or negative self-talk.

Self-compassion, in turn, strengthens our capacity to offer compassion to others. When we are kind and understanding toward ourselves, we are more likely to extend that same kindness to those around us. Compassion becomes a cycle: the more we practice it, the more it radiates outward, positively affecting our relationships and the world around us. In this way, compassion is not just an individual practice but a collective one. It can transform how we relate to others, view ourselves, and interact with the world.

Moreover, practicing compassion helps create a sense of shared humanity. We understand that suffering is a universal experience that connects us all. Whether it is physical pain, emotional turmoil, or mental distress, every human being experiences suffering at some point in their lives. When we recognize this shared experience, we are less likely to feel isolated in our struggles and more likely to reach out to others with empathy and care. This recognition of our shared humanity fosters a sense of belonging and community where individuals feel supported and understood.

Understanding Self-Compassion

While many people find it easy to extend compassion toward others, self-compassion can often be more difficult. This difficulty arises because many individuals are conditioned to hold to unrealistic standards, often engaging in harsh self-criticism when failing to meet them. However, just as we show kindness, care, and empathy to a friend or loved one facing hardship, it is equally essential to offer the same level of understanding to ourselves during times of struggle. Self-compassion is treating oneself with the same gentleness, patience, and care that one naturally offers to others in distress. As Dr. Kristin Neff, a pioneering researcher in self-compassion, explains, self-compassion involves three key components: self-kindness, common humanity, and mindfulness (Neff, 2003).

Self-kindness is the first component of self-compassion, and it involves offering oneself warmth, care, and understanding during moments of personal failure, challenge, or hardship. Instead of being harshly self-critical, self-kindness encourages individuals to respond to their imperfections and mistakes with the same encouragement and support they would give a close friend. For example, rather than chastising themselves for a perceived shortcoming, individuals practicing self-kindness might remind themselves that mistakes are a natural part of growth and learning. Self-kindness fosters an inner environment of acceptance and care, promoting emotional healing and resilience. It encourages people to speak to themselves with positive affirmations and supportive language rather than engaging in harsh self-talk that can damage self-esteem and mental well-being.

Common Humanity is the second core component of self-compassion. This aspect emphasizes recognizing that suffering, imperfection, and struggle are universal human experiences. It is easy to feel isolated in our suffering, believing we are the only ones facing failure, rejection, or hardship. However, self-compassion helps individuals realize that these experiences are a natural and unavoidable part of being human. Everyone encounters difficulties, and no one is immune to moments of vulnerability, disappointment, or inadequacy. By acknowledging the commonality of human suffering, individuals can overcome the sense of isolation and self-blame that often accompanies personal struggles. Instead, they can recognize that their experiences connect them to the broader human community, fostering a sense of shared understanding and empathy for themselves and others.

Mindfulness is the third key component of self-compassion and is crucial in fostering emotional balance. Mindfulness involves being fully present in the moment, observing one's thoughts, emotions, and sensations without judgment or attachment. When it comes to self-compassion, mindfulness allows individuals to acknowledge their painful emotions—such as sadness, frustration, or inadequacy—without becoming overwhelmed. It encourages a balanced perspective, where individuals neither suppress nor exaggerate their feelings. Through mindfulness, individuals can observe their emotional pain with curiosity and acceptance rather than reacting to it with harsh criticism or avoidance. This mindful awareness allows individuals to remain centered and grounded during difficult times, helping them cultivate a sense of inner calm and emotional stability.

These three components—self-kindness, common humanity, and mindfulness—create a robust framework for practicing self-compassion. By integrating these elements into daily life, individuals can transform their relationship with themselves, replacing self-judgment with self-acceptance and harsh criticism with understanding and care. The practice of self-compassion empowers individuals to approach their difficulties with grace and resilience, ultimately promoting greater emotional well-being.

Research has consistently demonstrated the psychological benefits of self-compassion. Numerous studies have shown that individuals who practice self-compassion experience greater emotional resilience, meaning they can better cope with life's challenges and bounce back from setbacks. For example, Neff et al. (2007) found that self-compassion was strongly linked to reduced levels of anxiety, depression, and stress, as well as increased life satisfaction and overall well-being. Individuals with higher levels of self-compassion were more likely to experience positive emotions, exhibit greater optimism, and maintain healthier interpersonal relationships.

In addition to promoting emotional resilience, self-compassion has been linked to healthier behaviors and improved self-care. When individuals treat themselves compassionately, they are more likely to engage in positive lifestyle choices supporting their physical and mental health. For instance, research by Breines and Chen (2012) found that self-compassionate individuals were more likely to adopt healthier eating habits, exercise regularly, and care for their mental health. They also demonstrated greater motivation for self-improvement, not out of inadequacy, but because they genuinely cared for their well-being.

Moreover, self-compassion has been shown to enhance motivation and personal growth. While some may worry that being self-compassionate will lead to complacency or a lack of ambition, the opposite is often true. Self-compassion fosters a supportive inner environment that encourages individuals to pursue their goals and strive for personal improvement without fearing failure. Self-compassionate individuals are more likely to take risks and persevere in the face of setbacks, as they are less likely to be paralyzed by self-doubt or fear of criticism. Instead of viewing failure as a reflection of their worth, self-compassionate individuals see it as an opportunity to learn and grow, allowing them to bounce back more quickly and continue working toward their goals.

Techniques for Cultivating Compassion

Cultivating compassion and self-compassion is a journey that requires intentional practice and dedication. Compassion, both for others and for oneself, is not always an innate response but rather a skill that can be developed over time. Mindfulness practices provide a robust framework for fostering compassion and helping individuals cultivate empathy, understanding, and kindness in their interactions with others and within themselves. There are several techniques rooted in mindfulness that are particularly effective in building and sustaining compassion, including loving-kindness meditation, compassionate breathing, and self-compassion journaling. These practices can be incorporated into daily routines to foster a habit of compassion and emotional resilience.

1. Loving-Kindness Meditation (Metta)

Loving-kindness meditation, or "Metta meditation," is one of the most well-known mindfulness practices for cultivating compassion. This practice involves generating feelings of warmth, kindness, and goodwill toward oneself and others by silently repeating phrases like, "May I be happy," "May I be healthy," and "May I be free from suffering." After focusing on oneself, the meditation expands outward, sending these exact wishes to loved ones, acquaintances, and eventually all beings. The goal is to build an emotional bridge of compassion that extends beyond the individual and touches everyone.

Research has shown that loving-kindness meditation can significantly increase positive emotions, including empathy and compassion, while reducing negative emotions, such as anger, stress, and fear (Hofmann et al., 2011). Studies have demonstrated that even short-term practice of loving-kindness meditation can lead to greater feelings of social connectedness and empathy, which are critical to building healthy relationships. Additionally, individuals who engage in regular loving-kindness meditation report improved emotional regulation and increased resilience when facing challenges.

This practice can also be beneficial for those who struggle with self-compassion. Often, people find it easier to extend kindness to others than themselves, and loving-kindness meditation offers a structured way to begin reversing this dynamic. By practicing self-directed phrases of love and goodwill, individuals can slowly dismantle harsh inner criticism and develop a more nurturing relationship with themselves. Over time, this practice can foster both emotional healing and a more compassionate outlook toward others.

2. Compassionate Breathing

Another effective mindfulness technique for cultivating compassion is compassionate breathing. This practice involves focusing on the breath while directing feelings of empathy and care toward oneself or another person. Compassionate breathing serves two primary purposes: it helps individuals stay grounded and centered in the present moment and encourages active cultivation of compassion. As people breathe deeply and mindfully, they are invited to envision sending waves of kindness, calm, and love to themselves or others.

This practice is beneficial in stressful or difficult situations where compassion might be overshadowed by frustration, anger, or fear. Research has demonstrated that focusing on the breath can activate the parasympathetic nervous system, responsible for the body's rest-and-digest response (Creswell et al., 2007). This process helps to reduce cortisol levels, lower blood pressure, and promote feelings of calm. The deep breathing, combined with the conscious intention of compassion, allows individuals to respond to situations from a place of empathy rather than reactivity.

For example, imagine encountering someone who is visibly upset or angry. Instead of reacting defensively, compassionate breathing offers the opportunity to pause, breathe, and bring a sense of calm to the interaction. By focusing on the breath and directing thoughts of empathy and understanding toward the person, the practice helps to diffuse emotional tension and allows for more compassionate communication. Similarly, when facing personal challenges, individuals can use compassionate breathing to soothe themselves and foster self-compassion, helping them navigate difficult emotions with greater ease and kindness.

3. Self-Compassion Journaling

Journaling has long been regarded as a valuable tool for self-reflection, emotional processing, and personal growth. When combined with self-compassion, journaling becomes an even more powerful practice. Self-compassion journaling involves writing about one's thoughts, emotions, and experiences while consciously offering oneself kindness and understanding. This practice allows individuals to explore their internal world without judgment, fostering a sense of self-acceptance and emotional healing.

To begin self-compassion journaling, individuals are encouraged to write about a specific challenge, failure, or complex emotion they are experiencing. Instead of focusing on self-criticism or judgment, they are asked to reflect on how they would respond if a friend or loved one were in the same situation. This exercise shifts the focus from negative self-talk to self-kindness, encouraging a more compassionate and supportive internal dialogue. Additionally, self-compassion journaling often includes the element of common humanity—recognizing that personal struggles are a universal part of the human experience and that no one is alone in their suffering.

Research has shown that self-compassion is associated with a range of psychological benefits, including increased emotional resilience, reduced anxiety and depression, and greater life satisfaction (Neff, 2003). Those who regularly engage in self-compassion practices, including journaling, are likelier to adopt healthier coping strategies and behaviors. Individuals develop a more nurturing and forgiving relationship with themselves by actively cultivating self-compassion, which ultimately enhances their well-being and interpersonal relationships.

4. Practicing Compassion in Daily Life

While structured practices like meditation and journaling are valuable, it is also essential to incorporate compassion into everyday interactions and routines. A straightforward way to do this is by setting daily intentions focused on compassion. For example, at the beginning of the day, individuals can take a moment to reflect on how they would like to show kindness and understanding toward others and themselves throughout the day. Whether offering a kind word to a colleague, listening deeply to a friend, or being patient with oneself, these small acts of compassion can profoundly impact overall well-being.

Another technique for integrating compassion into daily life is through mindful listening. In conversations, people are often more focused on what they will say next rather than truly hearing the other person. Mindful listening involves being fully present in the moment, actively listening to the speaker without judgment or interruption, and responding with empathy. This practice strengthens interpersonal relationships and helps create a compassionate and supportive environment in personal and professional settings.

Additionally, individuals can practice compassion by engaging in random acts of kindness, such as holding the door open for someone, offering a compliment, or helping a neighbor. Though seemingly simple, small gestures contribute to a culture of compassion and reinforce the habit of looking for opportunities to show kindness and care.

5. Building a Habit of Compassion

Cultivating compassion is not a one-time event but an ongoing process requiring consistent effort and practice. For this reason, it is essential to build compassion-focused practices into daily life to reinforce this mindset. Many people find it helpful to set aside time each day for practices like loving-kindness meditation or self-compassion journaling, ensuring that compassion remains an integral part of their routine.

Over time, these practices can become second nature, leading to more automatic responses of empathy and kindness in everyday situations. Studies have shown that individuals who engage in regular compassion-based practices experience long-lasting changes in brain function, particularly in areas associated with empathy and emotional regulation (Lutz et al., 2008). This suggests that compassion is not only a learned behavior but also one that can be deeply ingrained through mindfulness practice.

Additionally, participating in group meditation sessions, mindfulness retreats, or workshops focused on compassion can help reinforce these practices and provide a supportive community of like-minded individuals. Sharing experiences and insights with others on a similar journey can further deepen one's understanding and commitment to cultivating compassion.

Overcoming Barriers to Compassion

Overcoming barriers to compassion is essential to fully embracing its transformative potential. While compassion offers many benefits, such as enhanced relationships and emotional resilience, various obstacles can prevent individuals from tapping into this powerful practice. Often, these barriers stem from deeply ingrained beliefs about vulnerability, perfectionism, or the presence of an overly critical inner voice. Understanding and addressing these obstacles can help individuals move past them and incorporate compassion more freely into their lives.

1. Fear of Vulnerability

One of the most common barriers to compassion, particularly self-compassion, is the fear of vulnerability. Many people believe that showing kindness or empathy to themselves or others makes them susceptible to exploitation or judgment. The perception is that if they are too soft or lenient, others may take advantage of them or be seen as weak. This fear is especially prevalent in competitive environments, where strength and self-reliance are often prized over empathy.

However, research demonstrates that compassion is not a sign of weakness but a profound source of strength. Compassionate individuals are more likely to form strong, supportive relationships, which buffer against stress and emotional exhaustion. For instance, studies show that healthcare professionals who practice compassion are less likely to experience burnout despite working in high-stress environments (Keltner, 2009). Compassion fosters resilience by creating a supportive network that helps individuals navigate challenges without feeling overwhelmed or isolated.

Moreover, when individuals practice self-compassion, they allow themselves to be vulnerable without fearing judgment. They understand that being kind to themselves during difficult moments is not about excusing mistakes but about acknowledging their humanity. As Brené Brown famously noted, vulnerability is the birthplace of innovation, creativity, and change. By embracing vulnerability, individuals open themselves to personal growth and more profound, meaningful connections with others.

2. Perfectionism as a Barrier

Perfectionism is another major obstacle to developing self-compassion. Many individuals set impossibly high standards for themselves and experience intense self-criticism when they fail to meet these expectations. The belief that "I must be perfect" often leads to a cycle of judgment, shame, and emotional suffering. Perfectionists may find it difficult to practice self-compassion because they equate self-kindness with complacency. In their minds, being compassionate toward themselves might mean settling for mediocrity or giving up on their goals.

However, self-compassion does not mean lowering one's standards or avoiding self-improvement. Instead, it encourages a balanced perspective that allows individuals to recognize their efforts, even when they fall short. As Dr. Kristin Neff explains, self-compassion is about offering oneself understanding and support in the face of failure rather than harsh judgment (Neff, 2011). When individuals adopt a more compassionate mindset, they are more likely to persist in their efforts and show greater resilience in the face of setbacks.

Perfectionism can also prevent individuals from seeking help or admitting when struggling. The pressure to appear flawless often leads people to internalize their difficulties, exacerbating feelings of isolation and inadequacy. By practicing self-compassion, perfectionists can break free from these rigid expectations and embrace the idea that it is okay to be imperfect. This shift in mindset reduces stress and enhances motivation and creativity.

3. The Inner Critic

The inner critic, or the harsh internal voice that emerges during moments of difficulty or failure, is one of the most significant barriers to self-compassion. This inner voice often reinforces feelings of inadequacy, guilt, and shame, making it difficult for individuals to show themselves kindness. The inner critic may say things like, "You are not good enough," "You will never succeed," or "You are a failure." These negative thoughts can become deeply ingrained, making individuals believe they are unworthy of love, care, or compassion.

Mindfulness practices offer a powerful antidote to the inner critic by helping individuals recognize these thoughts without becoming overwhelmed. When individuals engage in mindfulness, they learn to observe their thoughts and emotions with curiosity and non-judgment. Rather than identifying with the inner critic, they can distance themselves from it and respond with self-compassion. Dr. Paul Gilbert, a leading expert in compassion-focused therapy, explains that mindfulness allows individuals to recognize that their inner critic is not an accurate reflection of their worth but rather a learned thinking pattern (Gilbert, 2009).

One effective technique for dealing with the inner critic is to practice compassionate dialogue. Instead of accepting the inner critic's harsh judgments, individuals can respond to themselves as they would to a distressed friend. For example, if the inner critic says, "You are a failure," the individual might respond, "It is okay to make mistakes. Everyone struggles sometimes, and I am doing my best." This shift in dialogue helps create a more supportive and nurturing internal environment, which promotes emotional healing and resilience.

4. Overcoming the Fear of Compassion

Sometimes, individuals may resist practicing compassion, fearing it will make them soft or complacent. They may worry that if they are too kind to themselves, they will lose their motivation or fail to achieve their goals. This fear is often rooted in a misunderstanding of what compassion truly means. Compassion is not about ignoring one's responsibilities or giving up on personal growth. Instead, it is about offering oneself kindness and support while striving for improvement.

Research has shown that individuals who practice self-compassion are likelier to engage in healthy behaviors and pursue their goals with incredible determination. Self-compassion is associated with higher levels of intrinsic motivation, meaning individuals are driven by a genuine desire to improve rather than by fear of failure or external validation (Breines & Chen, 2012). By offering compassion, individuals create a supportive inner environment fostering resilience and growth.

Overcoming the fear of compassion also involves reframing one's understanding of success. Rather than equating success with perfection or external achievement, individuals can begin to see success as a process of learning, growth, and self-improvement. This shift in perspective allows them to embrace compassion as a tool for long-term well-being rather than a hindrance to their goals.

5. Mindfulness as a Tool for Cultivating Compassion

Mindfulness plays a crucial role in overcoming barriers to compassion by helping individuals develop greater awareness of their thoughts, emotions, and behaviors. Individuals can observe their fears, perfectionism, and inner criticism through mindfulness without becoming entangled. This non-judgmental awareness allows individuals to respond to their challenges with compassion rather than reactivity.

For example, when individuals notice the inner critic arising, mindfulness allows them to pause and reflect before reacting. Instead of automatically accepting the critic's harsh judgments, they can respond with kindness and understanding. Similarly, mindfulness helps individuals recognize when they are holding themselves to unrealistic standards of perfectionism. By cultivating present-moment awareness, they can gently remind themselves that it is okay to be imperfect and that self-compassion is not a weakness.

Mindfulness practices such as loving-kindness meditation, compassionate breathing, and body scans are particularly effective in fostering compassion. These practices encourage individuals to connect with their emotions, cultivate empathy for themselves and others, and develop a more compassionate mindset. Over time, regular mindfulness practice can help individuals break free from the barriers that prevent them from fully embracing compassion.

Real-life examples provide robust evidence of the transformative effects of compassion and self-compassion. The following stories highlight how individuals from different walks of life have used mindfulness to cultivate compassion and improve their well-being.

- Caregivers and Compassion Fatigue: Caregivers often experience compassion fatigue and emotional and physical exhaustion caused by caring for others. One study by Raab (2014) found that practicing self-compassion helped caregivers reduce compassion fatigue and avoid burnout. By learning to care for themselves with the same kindness and understanding they offered to others, caregivers could maintain their emotional health and continue providing care without depleting their resources.

- Leaders and Empathetic Work Environments: Compassion in the workplace can lead to more robust team dynamics and improved job satisfaction. A case study of a corporate leader who incorporated mindfulness and compassionate leadership practices found that employees reported greater engagement, higher morale, and reduced stress (Boyatzis et al., 2006). The leader's commitment to fostering empathy and understanding created a supportive environment where employees felt valued and respected.

These stories demonstrate that compassion toward oneself and others can have far-reaching benefits in various contexts, from caregiving to corporate leadership.

As we reach the end of this chapter, it is time for you to pause and turn inward. Building self-compassion is not just about understanding the concept but about applying it to your everyday experiences. Start by taking a few quiet moments to reflect on your recent experiences and how you have spoken to yourself during challenging times. Ask yourself: "Was I kind to myself, or did I respond with harsh self-criticism?"

Self-Reflection Exercise

Begin with a simple journaling prompt: "Think of a recent moment when you felt disappointed in yourself. What thoughts did you have? How did you react? How might self-compassion have changed the way you experienced that moment?"

While reflecting, consider how you would respond to a friend going through the same situation. Would you criticize them, or would you offer understanding and encouragement? Please write down the words you would use to support a friend and then re-read them, directing them toward yourself. Imagine how it would feel to replace self-criticism with these words of kindness. Doing so trains your mind to adopt a more compassionate inner dialogue, transforming self-criticism into self-acceptance.

Personal Practice: Loving-Kindness Meditation

To deepen your experience of self-compassion, try incorporating a Loving-Kindness Meditation into your routine. Set aside a few minutes in a quiet space, sit comfortably, and close your eyes. Take a few deep breaths to center yourself. As you breathe, begin to repeat phrases silently.

- "May I be happy?"
- "May I be healthy?"
- "May I be free from suffering?"

Try to evoke feelings of warmth and kindness toward yourself with each repetition. If you notice any resistance or self-judgment, acknowledge it gently and return to the phrases. This exercise helps build a habit of extending love and compassion toward yourself and others, making it easier to approach difficult situations with an open heart.

Once you feel ready, expand the focus of the meditation to include others. Picture someone you care about silently repeating phrases such as:

- "May you be safe."
- "May you be peaceful."
- "May you be well."

This practice allows you to cultivate compassion for yourself and others, fostering a sense of interconnectedness and empathy.

Reflecting on the Impact

After completing the meditation, take a moment to journal about how you felt during and after the exercise. Did you find it challenging to offer yourself kindness? Were you able to extend compassion to others with more ease? Reflect on any emotions that arose and how this practice could influence how you respond to yourself and others daily.

By regularly engaging in self-reflection and compassion-building practices, you will begin to notice shifts in your perspective. You will likely become more patient with yourself, better able to navigate setbacks, and more open to extending kindness toward others. This approach nurtures your well-being and enhances the quality of your relationships.

Incorporating these reflective and meditative practices into your routine can help reinforce a mindset of self-compassion, leading to more resilience, emotional balance, and genuine self-care. Over time, self-compassion will naturally respond to life's challenges, providing a steady source of inner support and strength.

References:

- Boyatzis, R. E., Smith, M. L., & Blaize, N. (2006). Developing sustainable leaders through coaching and compassion. *Academy of Management Learning & Education, 5*(1), 8-24.
- Creswell, J. D., Way, B. M., Eisenberger, N. I., & Lieberman, M. D. (2007). Neural correlates of dispositional mindfulness during affect labeling. *Psychosomatic Medicine, 69*(6), 560-565.
- Dalai Lama. (2005). *The Compassionate Life*. Wisdom Publications.
- Gilbert, P. (2009). *The Compassionate Mind: A New Approach to Life's Challenges*. New Harbinger Publications.
- Gilbert, P., & Procter, S. (2006). Compassionate mind training for people with high shame and self-criticism: Overview and pilot study of a group therapy approach.

Clinical Psychology & Psychotherapy, 13(6), 353-379.

- Hofmann, S. G., Grossman, P., & Hinton, D. E. (2011). Loving-kindness and compassion meditation: Potential for psychological interventions. *Clinical Psychology Review, 31*(7), 1126-1132.
- Jazaieri, H., Jinpa, G. T., McGonigal, K., Rosenberg, E. L., Finkelstein, J., & Goldin, P. R. (2013). Enhancing compassion: A randomized controlled trial of a compassion cultivation training program. *Journal of Happiness Studies, 14*(4), 1113-1126.
- Keltner, D. (2009). *Born to Be Good: The Science of a Meaningful Life.* W. W. Norton & Company.
- Neff, K. D. (2003). The development and validation of a scale to measure self-compassion. *Self and Identity, 2*(3), 223–250.
- Neff, K. D. (2011). *Self-Compassion: The Proven Power of Being Kind to Yourself.* HarperCollins.
- Raab, K. (2014). Mindfulness, self-compassion, and empathy among health care professionals: A literature review. *Journal of Health Care Chaplaincy, 20*(3), 95–108.
- Salzberg, S. (2011). *Loving-Kindness: The Revolutionary Art of Happiness.* Shambhala Publications.

CHAPTER 11: THE ROLE OF GRATITUDE IN MINDFULNESS

Gratitude and Its Link to Well-Being

Gratitude is an emotion that goes far beyond saying "thank you" or acknowledging the good things in life in a fleeting moment. It is a deep, profound appreciation and recognition of everyday life's beauty, blessings, and abundance, regardless of the circumstances. Gratitude is transformative—it has the power to change our perspective, our emotional well-being, and even our physical health. Unlike other emotions that may come and go based on external situations, gratitude can be cultivated and developed into a constant mindset. By intentionally practicing gratitude, we shift our attention from what is lacking in life to what is plentiful. This focus on abundance rather than scarcity has been shown to improve overall well-being, increase happiness, and strengthen relationships.

Research on gratitude has consistently revealed its benefits on mental and emotional health. Studies by Emmons and McCullough (2003) demonstrated that individuals who regularly practice gratitude report higher positive emotions, more satisfaction with life, and greater optimism. Regularly acknowledging what we are thankful for has a powerful ripple effect on our mental state. When we focus on the good things in life, we naturally see more positive aspects of our experiences. This positive lens helps to reduce stress, alleviate symptoms of anxiety and depression, and create a more balanced emotional state.

Gratitude buffers against negative emotions such as envy, resentment, and regret. When grateful, we are less likely to compare ourselves to others or dwell on what we do not have. Instead, we cultivate a sense of contentment and peace, recognizing that what we already possess—relationships, health, or personal achievements—holds immense value. This shift in mindset reduces the tendency to focus on what is missing or imperfect, freeing us from the cycle of dissatisfaction that often leads to stress and unhappiness.

The practice of gratitude is deeply rooted in ancient traditions and philosophies. Philosophers such as Socrates, Marcus Aurelius, and Confucius all emphasized the importance of gratitude in living a fulfilled and meaningful life. Gratitude has long been considered a cornerstone of ethical and moral behavior. In religious and spiritual practices, gratitude is often seen as an expression of humility, reverence, and connection to a higher power. In many spiritual traditions, including Christianity, Buddhism, and Hinduism, gratitude is encouraged and viewed as a pathway to inner peace, enlightenment, and a deeper connection to the universe.

In modern times, psychologists and researchers have begun to study the science of gratitude, discovering that it is more than just a feel-good emotion. It is a tool that can be used to improve mental health, foster resilience, and enhance interpersonal relationships. The link between gratitude and well-being is clear: When we focus on the things we are thankful for, we become more mindful, more aware, and more present in our lives. This practice aligns perfectly with mindfulness, which also emphasizes living in the moment and accepting life as it is, without judgment.

Gratitude and mindfulness are two practices that complement each other beautifully. Mindfulness is being fully present and aware of your surroundings, thoughts, and emotions non-judgmentally. It encourages individuals to focus on the present moment rather than getting lost in past regrets or future anxieties. Gratitude enhances this practice by adding a layer of appreciation for the present moment. While mindfulness helps us stay grounded in the "now," gratitude helps us see the beauty, value, and goodness in that "now."

For example, imagine sitting outside in the early morning, feeling the cool breeze on your skin and hearing the birds sing. Mindfulness would guide you to observe these sensations and be present with them. Gratitude, on the other hand, would take it a step further by allowing you to appreciate the serenity of the moment—the peace of the morning, the beauty of nature, and the opportunity to experience this moment fully. Mindfulness and gratitude create a sense of completeness and fulfillment that enhances emotional well-being.

Moreover, both gratitude and mindfulness share a focus on acceptance. Mindfulness encourages acceptance of the present moment as it is, without resistance or judgment. Similarly, gratitude invites us to accept life as it comes, finding things to be thankful for even in challenging circumstances. It is easy to feel grateful when everything is going well, but genuine gratitude arises when we can appreciate the lessons, growth, and resilience from difficult times. This ability to find gratitude in hardship makes the practice so transformative—it helps us maintain perspective and stay connected to the positive aspects of life, no matter the external circumstances.

The benefits of gratitude are not limited to mental and emotional health; they also extend to physical well-being. Studies have shown that individuals who practice gratitude experience a wide range of physical health benefits, including improved immune function, better sleep, and lower levels of inflammation. Gratitude has been linked to lower blood pressure, reduced chronic pain symptoms, and a more remarkable ability to recover from illness (Seligman et al., 2005). One reason is that gratitude helps reduce the body's stress response. When stressed, our bodies release cortisol, which prepares us for "fight or flight." While this response is helpful in emergencies, chronic stress can lead to long-term health problems, such as heart disease, hypertension, and weakened immune function. Gratitude acts as a buffer against stress by encouraging relaxation, promoting positive emotions, and helping individuals stay grounded in the present moment. As a result, those who practice gratitude regularly experience lower cortisol levels and other stress-related hormones.

In addition to reducing stress, gratitude also promotes better sleep. Research has shown that individuals who practice gratitude are more likely to fall asleep faster, sleep longer, and wake up feeling refreshed. This is because gratitude shifts the mind from worrying thoughts to positive, peaceful reflections. By focusing on what they are thankful for before bed, individuals create a mental environment conducive to relaxation.

Gratitude also has a positive impact on heart health. Studies have shown that individuals who practice gratitude have lower levels of inflammation in the body, which is a significant risk factor for heart disease. By reducing stress and promoting positive emotions, gratitude helps protect the heart and improve overall cardiovascular health. This is especially important for individuals with chronic conditions such as hypertension or diabetes, as gratitude can help reduce the severity of symptoms and improve quality of life.

Gratitude has a profound effect on social relationships. Expressing gratitude strengthens our bonds with others, fosters trust, and creates a positive emotional atmosphere. Studies have shown that individuals who practice gratitude are more likely to engage in prosocial behavior, meaning that they are more likely to help others, show kindness, and act in ways that benefit their communities (Emmons & McCullough, 2003). This ripple effect of gratitude creates a culture of generosity and compassion where individuals feel supported and valued.

Expressing gratitude to others can also improve communication and reduce conflict. When we acknowledge the positive contributions of others, we create an environment of mutual respect and appreciation. This, in turn, fosters empathy and understanding, making it easier to resolve disagreements and build stronger, more fulfilling relationships. Gratitude is one of the most effective tools for improving romantic relationships, friendships, and workplace dynamics.

In addition to strengthening social bonds, gratitude also enhances emotional intelligence. When we practice gratitude, we become more attuned to the emotions of others, allowing us to respond with greater empathy and care. This increased emotional awareness improves our relationships and helps us navigate social situations with more grace and ease.

Section 2: Cultivating a Gratitude Mindset

Gratitude is a mindset that goes beyond simply expressing thanks for significant events or achievements; it is about learning to appreciate the small, everyday moments that might otherwise go unnoticed. Cultivating a gratitude mindset requires a conscious shift in focus—from what is lacking in life to what is already abundant. In many ways, this is the essence of mindfulness: being fully present in the moment and recognizing the goodness that already exists around us. While some people may naturally experience gratitude more efficiently, developing this mindset takes practice for most of us. Over time, however, with intentional effort, it can become an ingrained way of seeing the world, leading to greater contentment, happiness, and resilience.

One of the most effective tools for cultivating gratitude is the practice of **mindfulness-based gratitude journaling**. This involves setting aside a few moments each day to write down several things you are grateful for. The practice is often called the "Three Good Things" exercise, where individuals reflect on three positive experiences from their day. These can be small, simple things—a good conversation, the comfort of a warm bed, or even the joy of completing a task at work. While the concept seems simple, the power of gratitude journaling lies in its consistency. By regularly documenting moments of gratitude, we train our brains to focus on the positive aspects of life, which can rewire neural pathways and shift our overall mindset toward optimism. Studies have shown that individuals who engage in gratitude journaling report higher levels of well-being, improved mood, and reduced stress (Emmons, 2013).

When individuals commit to journaling their gratitude, they develop a heightened awareness of their daily experiences. This mindfulness practice increases appreciation for positive events and helps individuals find meaning and joy in moments they might have previously overlooked. For example, someone who practices gratitude journaling may come to appreciate the beauty of a sunset, the aroma of a morning coffee, or the sound of laughter with friends in a more profound way. Over time, these small, mindful reflections add up, creating a decisive shift in how one experiences and interacts with the world.

Gratitude Meditation: A Path to Connection and Inner Peace

Another powerful way to cultivate gratitude is through **mindfulness meditation** centered on appreciation. In gratitude meditation, individuals are invited to sit quietly, focus on their breath, and recall things or people they are grateful for. These meditations often begin with self-focused gratitude—appreciating the breath that sustains us, the body that carries us through the day, and the opportunities life has offered.

Gradually, the meditation can expand to include others—loved ones, friends, colleagues, or strangers who have positively impacted our lives. By intentionally sending thoughts of gratitude toward these individuals, we deepen our emotional bonds and foster a greater sense of connection and compassion.

Gratitude meditation can also be a source of inner peace, particularly in times of stress or difficulty. When faced with challenges, it is easy to become overwhelmed by negative emotions and lose sight of the good things that still exist in our lives. Practicing gratitude during these moments allows us to regain perspective. We can reduce stress and cultivate resilience by acknowledging what we are thankful for, even during hardship. This is not to minimize our difficulties but to remind ourselves that there is still beauty, kindness, and love to be found, even in tough times. Research has shown that gratitude meditation can lower anxiety levels, improve emotional regulation, and enhance well-being (Fredrickson, 2004).

Moreover, gratitude meditation can serve as a bridge to more profound mindfulness practices. Focusing on appreciation draws attention to the present moment, anchoring individuals in the here and now. This grounding effect allows practitioners to let go of future anxieties and past regrets, creating a state of calm and centeredness. As we become more aware of what we are grateful for, we also become more mindful of our thoughts, emotions, and physical sensations, further deepening our mindfulness practice. Over time, this practice can help individuals cultivate inner peace and stability beyond meditation and into their daily lives.

Building a Daily Gratitude Routine: Small Acts with Big Impact

In addition to formal practices like gratitude journaling and meditation, gratitude can be cultivated through small, mindful habits incorporated into daily life. Micro-practices of gratitude—those small moments where we pause and appreciate something—can be powerful in shifting our mindset over time. One simple yet effective way to do this is by setting daily reminders to pause and reflect on something we are grateful for. This can be as simple as appreciating a warm cup of tea in the morning, enjoying the sunlight streaming through a window, or feeling thankful for a moment of connection with a loved one. These brief pauses help anchor us in the present moment and reinforce a gratitude mindset.

Another effective technique is to create a gratitude ritual around specific activities. For example, before eating a meal, take a moment to express gratitude for the food in front of you—the farmers who grew it, the people who prepared it, and the nourishment it provides your body. Similarly, before going to bed, reflect on the day's events and consider at least one thing you are grateful for. By turning these ordinary moments into opportunities for gratitude, individuals can build a habit of mindfulness and appreciation that becomes second nature over time.

Even something as simple as expressing gratitude to others can profoundly impact both the giver and the receiver. A few moments to send a thank-you note, compliment someone or acknowledge a kind gesture can strengthen relationships and foster a sense of connection. Research has shown that people who regularly express gratitude to others report greater levels of happiness, improved relationships, and increased social support (Algoe et al., 2008). By regularly showing appreciation to those around us, we not only enhance their well-being but also deepen our sense of fulfillment.

The Ripple Effect of Gratitude: Transforming Communities and Cultures

As individuals develop a gratitude mindset, the benefits extend beyond their well-being. Gratitude has a **ripple effect**—expressing appreciation and kindness encourages others to do the same, creating a positive emotional atmosphere. This ripple effect can be seen in families, workplaces, and communities, where gratitude builds trust, reduces conflict, and fosters collaboration. In workplaces where gratitude is encouraged and practiced, employees report higher job satisfaction, more vital teamwork, and increased productivity (Grant & Gino, 2010). Similarly, families cultivating gratitude experience closer emotional bonds, greater resilience during challenges, and a more supportive home environment.

Gratitude can also play a role in **cultivating social justice and empathy**. When individuals practice gratitude, they are more likely to recognize their privileges and appreciate the contributions of others. This awareness fosters empathy, making individuals more attuned to the struggles of those around them. By acknowledging the support and kindness they receive, people are more likely to give back to their communities and engage in acts of service. In this way, gratitude enhances personal well-being and contributes to the greater good by creating a culture of generosity, compassion, and empathy.

The Science Behind Gratitude

Gratitude's impact on mental and physical health has been a significant focus in psychological and neuroscientific research. When we think about the simple act of expressing or receiving gratitude, it is easy to underestimate its profound and long-lasting effects on the brain and body. Neuroscientific evidence reveals that gratitude activates the brain's reward centers, triggering the release of crucial neurotransmitters such as dopamine and serotonin, which are associated with happiness and emotional well-being. When these chemicals are released, they foster feelings of connectedness, contentment, and optimism, enhancing our sense of community and belonging (Zahn et al., 2009).

The brain's "reward system" essentially reinforces behaviors promoting survival and well-being. Gratitude, when practiced regularly, becomes one of these positive reinforcement mechanisms, encouraging us to recognize and focus on the good in our lives. Whether we are grateful for a friend's support, the beauty of nature, or small acts of kindness, these moments spark the brain's reward system, making it more likely that we will continue to seek out and focus on experiences that make us feel thankful.

More importantly, consistent gratitude practice leads to structural changes in the brain. Research suggests that people who regularly practice gratitude experience increased neural activity in the medial prefrontal cortex—a region involved in decision-making, social cognition, and emotional regulation. In a study published in *Social Cognitive and Affective Neuroscience*, Fox et al. (2015) demonstrated that this area of the brain becomes more engaged when people reflect on things they are grateful for. This enhanced neural sensitivity helps individuals manage their emotions more effectively, allowing them to navigate life's challenges with a more balanced and positive mindset. As the brain becomes more accustomed to focusing on the positive, it becomes easier to manage negative emotions, reducing the overall intensity of stress, anxiety, and fear.

Gratitude's Long-Term Effects on Mental Health

While short-term expressions of gratitude boost happiness and feelings of well-being, the long-term benefits of a consistent gratitude practice are even more profound. According to psychological studies, gratitude significantly reduces symptoms of depression and anxiety. Depression often arises from negative thinking patterns—rumination on past events, feelings of worthlessness, or hopelessness about the future. Gratitude, by shifting the focus toward what is good in the present, interrupts these negative cycles of thought.

A study published in *Clinical Psychology Review* found that gratitude interventions significantly reduced symptoms of depression in participants, leading to higher life satisfaction and emotional well-being (Wood et al., 2010). This effect occurs because gratitude promotes a more balanced cognitive perspective, helping individuals acknowledge their challenges and strengths, successes, and support systems. Gratitude fosters a sense of resilience, allowing individuals to cope more effectively with stressors and setbacks.

Additionally, gratitude has been shown to improve emotional regulation, helping individuals manage difficult emotions like anger, frustration, and sadness more constructively. Regularly practicing gratitude makes individuals less likely to become overwhelmed by negative emotions as they learn to focus on the positive aspects of their experiences. This does not mean ignoring or suppressing negative feelings but instead developing the capacity to see both sides of a situation —acknowledging pain while recognizing hope, support, and positive outcomes.

Physical Health Benefits: A Mind-Body Connection

The benefits of gratitude extend beyond mental well-being, positively influencing physical health. Research has shown that individuals who regularly practice gratitude experience lower blood pressure, improved immune function, and better cardiovascular health. One reason for this is that gratitude reduces stress, which is known to have detrimental effects on the body. Chronic stress leads to the prolonged release of cortisol, a hormone associated with the "fight-or-flight" response, which, when elevated for extended periods, can weaken the immune system, raise blood pressure, and contribute to heart disease. Gratitude, by promoting positive emotional states, helps counteract these harmful physiological effects by engaging the parasympathetic nervous system—the "rest and digest" system responsible for recovery and relaxation.

People who practice gratitude tend to experience lower levels of inflammation, a critical factor in many chronic illnesses, including heart disease, diabetes, and autoimmune disorders. Research suggests that this reduction in inflammation may be related to gratitude's ability to lower stress hormones and enhance immune function. Studies have also demonstrated that people who practice gratitude are likelier to engage in healthy behaviors, such as regular exercise, a balanced diet, and getting enough sleep. These behaviors, in turn, contribute to better overall physical health (Emmons & McCullough, 2003).

Gratitude and Its Role in Enhancing Sleep and Reducing Physical Pain

Gratitude's impact on sleep is another area of interest in scientific research. Poor sleep is often linked to higher levels of stress and anxiety, as individuals struggle to "turn off" their racing thoughts before bed. Gratitude, however, has been shown to improve sleep quality by promoting more positive thinking before bedtime. A study published in *Applied Psychology: Health and Well-Being* found that participants who practiced gratitude exercises before bed reported falling asleep faster, sleeping longer, and experiencing higher sleep quality (Wood et al., 2009). By focusing on what went well during the day, rather than worrying about what might go wrong tomorrow, gratitude allows the mind to rest and reduces pre-sleep anxiety, leading to a more restful night.

Gratitude can also play a significant role in managing chronic pain. Pain, whether physical or emotional, is often exacerbated by negative thinking patterns, including catastrophizing or focusing on what is wrong. By practicing gratitude, individuals can shift their focus from the pain to the aspects of life that bring joy, comfort, and meaning. A study published in *Personality and Individual Differences* found that gratitude was associated with lower levels of pain perception and increased pain tolerance (Hill et al., 2013). While gratitude does not eliminate pain, it changes how individuals experience it, allowing them to maintain a sense of well-being despite physical discomfort.

Creating a Positive Feedback Loop: The Cycle of Gratitude

One of the most remarkable aspects of gratitude is its ability to create a **positive feedback loop**. As individuals practice gratitude, they notice more things to be grateful for, reinforcing positive emotions and behaviors. The brain becomes more attuned to positive experiences, making it easier to recognize and appreciate them in the future. This cycle creates a snowball effect, where the more gratitude individuals express, the more benefits they experience, both mentally and physically.

This positive feedback loop extends to relationships as well. People who regularly express gratitude are more likely to strengthen their relationships, as gratitude fosters feelings of appreciation, trust, and connection. When individuals feel valued and appreciated, they are more likely to reciprocate those feelings, creating a cycle of positive reinforcement in relationships. This is why gratitude is often called a "social glue"—it strengthens bonds, reduces conflict, and enhances feelings of closeness and empathy.

In conclusion, gratitude is far more than a fleeting feeling; it is a powerful practice that can transform mental and physical health. By consistently practicing gratitude, individuals can rewire their brains to focus on the positive, manage stress more effectively, improve emotional regulation, and experience better physical health. The benefits of gratitude extend beyond personal well-being, influencing relationships, communities, and even the broader social fabric. As more research emerges on the science of gratitude, it becomes increasingly clear that this simple practice has the potential to change lives for the better.

Overcoming Challenges in Practicing Gratitude

Overcoming challenges in practicing gratitude is a significant aspect of maintaining emotional well-being, mainly when life throws unexpected difficulties. While gratitude is widely recognized for its ability to boost mental health, it can sometimes feel elusive, especially when faced with stress, hardship, or adversity. During these times, the practice of gratitude can feel most distant, yet ironically, it is in these moments that gratitude has the potential to offer the most profound healing. By cultivating mindfulness, individuals can overcome common barriers to gratitude, such as negativity bias, feelings of resentment, and emotional overwhelm.

One of the most deeply ingrained barriers to practicing gratitude is the mind's natural tendency to dwell on the negative—a phenomenon known as the negativity bias. This evolutionary trait has helped humans survive by making us more attuned to potential threats and dangers. However, in modern life, this bias can lead us to focus more on what is going wrong than what is going right, making gratitude feel like a distant emotion. The mind becomes fixated on stressful situations, mistakes, or disappointments, and even the good things in life are often overshadowed. Research shows that this bias can cloud our ability to recognize positive experiences, even when they are present.

Mindfulness offers a powerful antidote to this pattern by increasing awareness of our thoughts and mental habits. When individuals become mindful of their thoughts, they can identify the negativity bias in action and actively work to shift their focus. Instead of being swept away by negative emotions, mindfulness invites people to observe their thoughts non-judgmentally. By acknowledging the presence of negativity, individuals can consciously redirect their attention toward gratitude, even if it takes practice. This shift does not mean forcing a positive mindset but creating space for positive and negative experiences. Over time, individuals who engage in mindfulness find that they can more easily notice and appreciate the good in life despite the brain's natural tendency to focus on the bad.

Another common barrier to gratitude is the misconception that gratitude downplays real struggles or hardships. Some individuals resist practicing gratitude because they feel it is unrealistic or dismissive of their pain. This perspective, however, needs to understand the true nature of gratitude. Gratitude does not require individuals to ignore their challenges or pretend everything is perfect. Instead, it invites them to hold a broader perspective, acknowledging that there is still something to appreciate even during tough times. This is where mindfulness plays a critical role. By fostering a mindset of acceptance, mindfulness allows individuals to hold space for difficult emotions and moments of gratitude.

For example, someone going through a tough time might need help to focus on large-scale blessings. In these moments, practicing "micro-gratitude" can be especially helpful. This involves finding gratitude in small, simple moments—a warm cup of tea, a stranger's smile, or the feeling of sunshine on your face. By focusing on these tiny moments of positivity, individuals can build a foundation for tremendous gratitude without dismissing the genuine difficulties they are experiencing. Over time, these small acts of gratitude compound, creating a more resilient and grateful mindset.

Resentment is another barrier that can block gratitude. When individuals harbor resentment—whether towards others, themselves, or life circumstances—it can be challenging to tap into a sense of thankfulness. Resentment clouds the ability to see the good, focusing instead on past hurts, grievances, or perceived injustices. In this state, gratitude might feel out of reach, but mindfulness can provide a way forward.

By practicing mindful acceptance, individuals can begin to let go of resentment by observing their feelings without becoming attached to them. Rather than suppressing or denying feelings of resentment, mindfulness invites individuals to sit with their emotions, notice where they feel them in their bodies, and breathe through the discomfort. This process allows them to release some of the emotional weight, creating room for gratitude to re-enter. By approaching emotions mindfully, individuals can move beyond resentment and reconnect with appreciation for the positive aspects of their lives.

During particularly stressful or overwhelming periods, it can be helpful to incorporate mindful breathing and grounding exercises to support a gratitude practice. These techniques calm the nervous system, helping individuals slow down and reconnect with the present moment. Mindful breathing involves taking slow, deep breaths while paying attention to the sensation of the breath entering and leaving the body. As the breath slows, so does the mind, creating space for clarity and appreciation. Grounding exercises, such as focusing on physical sensations or tuning in to the sights and sounds of the environment, can also bring individuals back to the present, helping them recognize the beauty in their immediate surroundings.

Incorporating gratitude into daily life during stressful periods can also be achieved through gratitude journaling or a daily gratitude ritual. Individuals can train their minds to seek out and recognize positivity by writing down three things they are grateful for daily. This simple yet powerful exercise helps build mental resilience by creating a pattern of appreciation, even when life feels challenging. Over time, gratitude journaling has rewired the brain, making focusing on the positive aspects of life and enhancing mental well-being easier.

Guided gratitude meditations may also be helpful for individuals struggling with overwhelming emotions or stress. These meditations focus on cultivating a sense of appreciation for one's body, mind, and experiences, regardless of whether they are positive or negative. By guiding individuals through the process of expressing gratitude, even during challenging times, these meditations can help reduce feelings of stress and promote a more balanced emotional state.

Another mindfulness technique that supports gratitude during adversity is "savoring." Savoring involves slowing down and fully immersing oneself in positive experiences as they happen. By intentionally focusing on the richness of these moments—whether it's enjoying a meal, spending time with loved ones, or appreciating nature—individuals can deepen their sense of gratitude. Savoring allows them to not only recognize positive experiences but also fully absorb and enjoy them, creating lasting emotional benefits.

Building resilience through gratitude is not a quick fix but a practice that grows stronger over time. Individuals can gradually develop a more robust gratitude practice by starting small and incorporating mindfulness techniques into daily life. Even during tough times, gratitude becomes a tool for maintaining emotional balance, allowing individuals to see beyond their current difficulties and recognize the good in their lives. As mindfulness and gratitude work together, individuals can cultivate a deep appreciation, leading to greater resilience, well-being, and inner peace.

Real-life stories can provide deep and powerful insights into how the practice of gratitude can transform not only a person's mental and emotional well-being but also their physical health. Gratitude, when consistently practiced, has the potential to bring about profound shifts in one's outlook on life, promoting resilience, joy, and a deeper connection to oneself and others. In this section, we will explore the journeys of several individuals who have embraced gratitude, highlighting how this practice has led to meaningful changes.

One compelling case is that of Marie, a cancer survivor who went through grueling rounds of chemotherapy and radiation. At first, Marie felt overwhelmed by the physical pain, exhaustion, and emotional toll of her diagnosis. Depression and anxiety weighed heavily on her as she faced uncertainty about her future. However, after being introduced to gratitude journaling by a friend, she began documenting the small things she was thankful for each day. Initially, her entries were simple, such as feeling grateful for the fresh air or a supportive conversation with a loved one. Over time, this daily practice expanded as Marie noticed and appreciated more aspects of her life, from the beauty of a sunset to her body's strength in recovery. Gratitude helped her reframe her experience—while her illness was undeniably brutal, she found moments of light and hope. As her mindset shifted, she also noticed improvements in her emotional resilience, making her more equipped to handle the challenges of treatment. Through gratitude, Marie cultivated a sense of peace, which contributed to her healing process and helped her maintain a sense of hope throughout her journey.

Another powerful story is that of James, a high-powered corporate executive who, after years of working in a fast-paced environment, began to experience severe burnout. The constant stress, coupled with long hours, took a toll on both his mental health and his relationships with his team and family. James became increasingly irritable, fatigued, and disconnected from the people and activities he once enjoyed. After recognizing the toll that burnout had on his life, James attended a mindfulness retreat where he learned about gratitude. One of the daily exercises was to express appreciation to someone in his life, whether for a kind gesture or simply being there. James began by writing short notes of gratitude to his colleagues and family, expressing appreciation for their support and collaboration. As this practice became more ingrained in his routine, James noticed a remarkable shift in his mood and energy levels and the dynamics of his work environment. His relationships with his team members improved as he fostered a more positive, supportive atmosphere. Gratitude helped James reconnect with his purpose and reignited his passion for his career while promoting better work-life balance.

Samantha, a young mother, struggled with postpartum depression after the birth of her second child. The overwhelming demands of motherhood, combined with feelings of inadequacy and isolation, left her emotionally depleted. After reading about the benefits of gratitude in managing stress and depression, she decided to incorporate a nightly gratitude practice into her routine. Each evening, after her children were asleep, Samantha would spend a few moments reflecting on the day and jotting down three things she was grateful for, no matter how small. Her gratitude list sometimes included simple pleasures, like a warm cup of tea or a smile from her baby. On other days, it was more profound —like appreciating her body for carrying and nurturing her children or feeling grateful for her partner's support. Over time, Samantha's gratitude practice became a lifeline, helping her shift her focus away from the difficulties of new motherhood and toward the joys, however small, that each day offered. As she cultivated gratitude, Samantha began to feel more grounded, resilient, and connected to her role as a mother, eventually noticing a reduction in her symptoms of depression.

These stories illustrate that gratitude, when practiced mindfully, has the potential to transform lives in powerful ways. Whether in the face of illness, burnout, or emotional struggles, gratitude is a tool for reframing difficult experiences, fostering resilience, and creating a more positive outlook. It reminds individuals to focus on the present moment, to recognize the good that exists, and to cultivate a sense of peace and fulfillment, even in challenging times.

Reflection and Personal Practice

Integrating gratitude into daily mindfulness is essential to harnessing its powerful transformative power. While gratitude may seem simple, intentionally practicing it requires consistent effort and reflection. This section will explore several reflective exercises and journaling prompts designed to help individuals cultivate a deeper sense of gratitude in their everyday lives.

One of the most effective exercises is gratitude journaling, which encourages individuals to reflect on three things they are grateful for daily. This can be done in the morning, setting a positive tone for the day ahead or in the evening to reflect on the day's events. By focusing on the positive aspects of life—no matter how small—gratitude journaling helps shift attention away from stressors, fostering a greater sense of contentment over time. Readers are encouraged to begin this practice with the prompt: "What are three things, big or small, that I am grateful for today?" With regular practice, individuals will notice a shift in their mindset, making recognizing and appreciating the good moments easier, even on challenging days.

Another powerful exercise is a gratitude meditation, which guides individuals through cultivating appreciation for the present moment. In this meditation, individuals can focus on their breath, body, and immediate surroundings. They are encouraged to express gratitude for each breath, their body's strength and resilience, and the people, opportunities, and experiences enriching their lives. This meditation can be practiced daily to foster a deeper connection to oneself and the world. By practicing gratitude in this way, individuals can deepen their mindfulness practice and enhance their overall sense of peace and contentment.

In addition to journaling and meditation, readers can explore gratitude affirmations, simple phrases that remind them to appreciate life's blessings. For example, affirmations like "I am grateful for the abundance in my life" or "I appreciate the support and love of those around me" can be repeated throughout the day to reinforce a gratitude mindset. Whether spoken aloud or written down, these affirmations are powerful tools for redirecting attention toward positivity and away from negative thoughts.

Readers are also encouraged to incorporate acts of gratitude into their daily lives. These acts can be as simple as sending a thank-you note, expressing appreciation to a colleague, or doing something kind for a loved one. By actively expressing gratitude, individuals can deepen their connections with others and cultivate a sense of joy and fulfillment. Acts of gratitude improve relationships and contribute to a more positive and compassionate mindset, creating a ripple effect that extends beyond the individual.

Gratitude is a transformative practice that complements mindfulness by grounding individuals in the present moment and fostering a more positive outlook. The consistent practice of gratitude can improve mental, emotional, and physical well-being through journaling, meditation, affirmations, or acts of gratitude. It invites individuals to appreciate the beauty of the present, to let go of negativity, and to cultivate a mindset of abundance and joy. Over time, gratitude can become a powerful tool for navigating life's challenges with resilience, fostering deeper connections with others, and experiencing greater fulfillment and peace. By integrating gratitude into daily mindfulness practice, individuals can create a rich life with appreciation, positivity, and contentment.

References:

- Emmons, R. A., & McCullough, M. E. (2003). Counting blessings versus burdens: An experimental investigation of gratitude and subjective well-being in daily life. *Journal of Personality and Social Psychology, 84*(2), 377–389.
- Fox, G. R., Kaplan, J., Damasio, H., & Damasio, A. (2015). Neural correlates of gratitude. *Frontiers in Psychology, p. 6*, 1491.
- Seligman, M. E. P., Steen, T. A., Park, N., & Peterson,

C. (2005). Positive psychology progress: Empirical validation of interventions. *American Psychologist, 60*(5), 410-421.

- Wood, A. M., Froh, J. J., & Geraghty, A. W. (2010). Gratitude and well-being: A review and theoretical integration. *Clinical Psychology Review, 30*(7), 890-905.
- Zahn, R., Garrido, G., Moll, J., & Grafman, J. (2009). Individual differences in posterior cortical volume and appreciative traits predict gratitude responses: Behavioral and brain-based correlates. *Social Cognitive and Affective Neuroscience, 4*(3), 273-284.

CHAPTER 12: MINDFULNESS IN THE WORKPLACE

Why Mindfulness Matters at Work

The workplace is often one of the most significant sources of stress for individuals in modern society. With constant deadlines, meetings, and an ever-growing list of responsibilities, employees frequently struggle to maintain mental clarity and emotional balance. Mindfulness in the workplace has gained increasing attention as a solution to these challenges, offering a way to reduce stress, improve focus, and foster better communication among colleagues (Good et al., 2016).

Mindfulness is defined as paying attention to the present moment intentionally and without judgment (Kabat-Zinn, 1990). In the workplace, this means being fully present in each task, whether listening actively during a meeting or focusing solely on a project without being distracted by thoughts of upcoming tasks. When individuals practice mindfulness at work, they enhance their ability to manage distractions, make thoughtful decisions, and navigate stressful situations more easily.

Research supports the idea that mindfulness can enhance workplace outcomes. A study published in *Mindfulness* found that employees who practiced mindfulness experienced lower stress levels and higher job satisfaction (Hülsheger et al., 2013). Additionally, practicing mindfulness has been linked to improvements in emotional intelligence, which helps individuals better understand and manage their emotions and empathize with others (Goleman, 1998). These improvements in emotional regulation can lead to more harmonious working relationships and better team dynamics.

Mindfulness also helps enhance focus and productivity, two areas often compromised by workplace stress. A study from the *Journal of Occupational Health Psychology* revealed that employees who engaged in mindfulness exercises reported increased focus and cognitive performance (Dane & Brummel, 2014). With the growing demand for multitasking and the ever-present digital distractions, maintaining focus has become an essential skill in the workplace. Mindfulness can teach individuals to focus on one task at a time, ultimately improving productivity.

In summary, mindfulness matters in the workplace because it addresses key challenges such as stress, lack of focus, and communication breakdowns. Employees can enhance their well-being and foster a more collaborative, productive work environment by practicing mindfulness.

Mindfulness Techniques for Productivity

Mindfulness is a powerful tool that can significantly enhance productivity by fostering focus, clarity, and better time management. In today's fast-paced work environments, distractions and multitasking often impede efficiency, leading to stress, mental fatigue, and burnout. However, by incorporating mindfulness techniques into daily routines, individuals can cultivate a more focused, engaged, and productive mindset, helping them to perform at their best while maintaining balance. Let us explore several mindfulness techniques that can significantly boost productivity.

One of the most effective methods for improving productivity is mindful task prioritization. This technique encourages individuals to take time each morning to consciously assess and rank their daily tasks, determining which ones are most critical to accomplish. This practice clarifies the day's priorities and helps reduce the overwhelming feeling of having too many tasks. Research supports that task prioritization is critical to enhancing productivity because it allows people to concentrate their mental and physical energy on activities that yield the most significant results (Levy & Wobbrock, 2015). By being mindful of which tasks should come first, individuals can allocate their best energy toward high-impact projects, ultimately leading to a more streamlined and effective workflow.

To engage in mindful task prioritization, begin by creating a list of all the tasks that need to be completed. Then, pause and reflect on which tasks are most important because of deadlines, potential impact, or alignment with larger goals. Rather than rushing to complete less meaningful tasks for a quick sense of accomplishment, focus on those that will make the most significant difference. Practicing mindful prioritization helps ensure that individuals work strategically, not just reactively. It fosters a sense of control over one's workload and boosts efficiency by minimizing time spent on low-priority distractions.

Another proven technique that boosts productivity is focused work intervals, such as the Pomodoro Technique. The Pomodoro Technique involves working in short, highly focused bursts of 25 minutes, followed by a 5-minute break. After four cycles, or "Pomodoros," a longer break of 15-30 minutes is taken. This approach combines mindfulness with time management by helping individuals stay present and fully engaged in a task for a set period, knowing they have a designated break coming.

The key is avoiding distractions during the work interval and focusing solely on the task. By breaking work into manageable chunks, individuals can avoid feeling overwhelmed, reduce mental fatigue, and maintain steady productivity throughout the day. Studies have found that using focused work intervals improves concentration, supports better time management, and enhances overall performance (Cirillo, 2006).

In addition to work intervals, taking mindful breaks is crucial for sustaining high productivity levels throughout the day. The brain is not designed to focus for extended periods without rest, and pushing through long hours without breaks can diminish performance. Mindful breaks, which could be as simple as a few minutes of mindful breathing or stepping away from the desk to stretch, provide an opportunity for the mind to rest, recharge, and reset. Research shows that employees who take regular breaks—particularly every 90 minutes—are more productive and maintain higher cognitive performance levels than those who work for longer stretches without rest (Caldwell et al., 2001). Incorporating mindful activities into these breaks, such as a brief body scan, breathing exercises, or a short walk, allows individuals to reconnect with their bodies, release tension, and return to work with renewed focus and clarity.

Another mindfulness-based productivity tool is single-task focus, which encourages individuals to focus on one task at a time rather than multitasking. Multitasking may seem efficient, but research has shown that it can reduce productivity by up to 40% as the brain struggles to switch between tasks and maintain focus (Rosen, 2008). Mindfulness trains the mind to remain fully present with one activity, allowing individuals to give their undivided attention to each task. This practice improves the quality of work and speeds up completion time because the individual is not constantly distracted by other competing demands. Single-tasking is especially valuable in today's work environments, where digital distractions like emails, notifications, and phone calls are constant. By setting boundaries around work time and focusing on one task at a time, employees can increase their productivity and reduce feelings of mental exhaustion.

To implement single-task focus, consider setting specific time blocks during the day for different tasks. During these blocks, turn off notifications and focus entirely on the task, whether writing, responding to emails, or attending a meeting. When the task is complete or the time block ends, take a brief mindful break before moving on to the next task. This approach helps individuals stay organized, minimizes the mental strain of juggling multiple priorities, and enhances the overall quality of work.

In addition to these techniques, mindful time management is another practice that can improve productivity. Time management is a critical skill in any professional setting, and mindfulness can play a significant role in helping individuals manage their time more effectively. By being mindful of how time is spent, individuals can identify unproductive habits, such as procrastination or overcommitment, and take steps to improve their efficiency. Mindful time management involves planning the day intentionally, setting realistic goals, and knowing how each minute is used. For example, individuals might allocate specific periods for high-focus work, collaborative meetings, and personal breaks, ensuring that all aspects of the day are accounted for. A mindful approach to time helps individuals stay organized, reduces stress, and allows for a more balanced workflow.

Another helpful tool in mindful time management is the digital detox—setting aside times during the day when all digital distractions are minimized. This can include turning off email notifications, silencing the phone, or using apps that block social media during work hours. By creating designated times for checking emails or engaging in digital communication, individuals can avoid the constant pull of notifications and focus entirely on their work. This helps to prevent distractions and fosters a more mindful, intentional use of time throughout the day.

Incorporating mindfulness into productivity also involves creating a mindful workspace. A cluttered, chaotic workspace can lead to mental overwhelm and reduced productivity, while a clean, organized space promotes clarity and focus. Mindfulness encourages individuals to pay attention to their environment and make intentional changes that enhance their ability to work efficiently. This might involve organizing files, decluttering the desk, and creating a calming atmosphere with minimal distractions. By cultivating a workspace that supports mindfulness, individuals are better able to maintain focus and work effectively.

Managing Stress and Burnout

Stress and burnout are increasingly prevalent issues in the modern workplace, especially in fast-paced industries where employees are expected to maintain high levels of productivity under constant pressure. The demands of meeting deadlines, achieving performance goals, and juggling multiple tasks often lead to chronic stress, eventually resulting in burnout. As defined by researchers Maslach and Leiter (2016), burnout is a state of emotional exhaustion, depersonalization (a sense of detachment from one's work or colleagues), and a reduced sense of personal accomplishment. It is a global health concern affecting millions of workers, causing a decline in mental and physical health, organizational productivity, and employee retention.

In this context, mindfulness has emerged as a powerful tool for preventing and managing burnout. Mindfulness practices help individuals cultivate greater emotional resilience, self-awareness, and coping with stress before it escalates. Burnout does not happen overnight; it builds up gradually as stress accumulates and is left unaddressed. With the consistent application of mindfulness techniques, individuals can recognize the early signs of burnout, such as fatigue, irritability, or a lack of enthusiasm for work, and take appropriate steps to mitigate its impact.

One of the key benefits of mindfulness is its ability to help individuals recognize the early signs of stress before it becomes overwhelming. Mindfulness involves tuning into the present moment and paying attention to physical and emotional sensations. In a workplace setting, this can mean noticing when muscle tension, headaches, or fatigue arise—physical indicators that stress levels are increasing. When individuals become more aware of these subtle signs, they can take proactive steps to manage their stress, such as taking a short break, practicing mindful breathing, or engaging in a quick mindfulness exercise. This early intervention is crucial in preventing stress from escalating into burnout.

One effective mindfulness technique for managing stress is Mindfulness-Based Stress Reduction (MBSR). Developed by Dr. Jon Kabat-Zinn in the 1970s, MBSR is a structured program that combines mindfulness meditation and body awareness exercises to reduce stress and improve overall well-being. MBSR includes breathwork, mindful movement (e.g., yoga or walking meditation), and body scanning. In a body scan meditation, individuals systematically bring their attention to different parts of their bodies, noticing sensations without judgment. This practice is particularly effective in releasing physical tension, calming the nervous system, and promoting relaxation. By regularly engaging in body scanning, employees can address physical and mental stress in real time, preventing it from accumulating and leading to burnout.

Research has consistently demonstrated the effectiveness of MBSR in workplace settings. A study published in The Journal of Occupational Health Psychology found that employees who practiced MBSR techniques experienced significant reductions in perceived stress levels and improved sleep quality, mood, and overall well-being (Wolever et al., 2012). This suggests that mindfulness helps individuals cope with stress in the moment and fosters long-term resilience by rewiring the brain to respond more calmly to future stressors. By making mindfulness a regular part of their routine, employees can enhance their capacity to handle workplace challenges without feeling overwhelmed.

Another essential aspect of preventing burnout is cultivating emotional resilience—the ability to bounce back from setbacks and face challenges with a calm and composed mindset. Emotional resilience does not mean avoiding stress altogether; instead, it involves managing stress effectively and recovering quickly from difficult situations. Mindfulness strengthens emotional resilience by teaching individuals to observe their thoughts and emotions without becoming entangled. For example, when faced with a high-pressure project or a demanding client, a mindful employee can take a step back, acknowledge their stress without judgment, and choose how to respond thoughtfully rather than impulsively. This practice, known as "response flexibility," enables individuals to handle stressful situations with greater clarity and composure.

In addition to promoting emotional resilience, mindfulness can help individuals cultivate self-compassion, which is particularly important for preventing burnout. Many employees, particularly those who are perfectionistic or have a strong sense of responsibility, are prone to self-criticism when they fall short of their goals or face challenges. This internal pressure can exacerbate stress and contribute to feelings of inadequacy, leading to burnout over time. Self-compassion, as defined by Dr. Kristin Neff (2011), involves treating oneself with the same kindness, care, and understanding that one would offer to a friend during times of difficulty. By practicing self-compassion, individuals can develop a more balanced and forgiving relationship with themselves, which reduces the risk of burnout.

Self-compassion can be fostered through simple mindfulness exercises such as compassionate breathing, where individuals focus on their breath while silently offering themselves kind and supportive words. For example, during a stressful moment, an employee might repeat to themselves, "It is okay to feel overwhelmed right now. I am doing the best I can." This practice helps counteract the harsh inner critic and promotes a more supportive and understanding internal dialogue. Over time, self-compassion strengthens emotional resilience by helping individuals maintain a sense of self-worth despite setbacks or failures.

Furthermore, mindfulness encourages individuals to cultivate healthy boundaries between work and personal life, essential for preventing burnout. In today's always-connected work environment, many employees struggle to "switch off" after hours, leading to constant mental and emotional strain. By practicing mindfulness, individuals can become more aware of the importance of work-life balance and set clear boundaries to protect their well-being. This might involve creating designated times for rest, practicing mindful transitions between work and home life, or setting limits on after-hours work communication.

Building Mindful Leadership

Mindfulness is not only beneficial for employees but also plays a crucial role in shaping effective leadership. Mindful leadership involves leading with heightened awareness, emotional intelligence, and compassion. Leading mindfully is more critical than ever in today's fast-paced and often high-pressure corporate environments. Mindful leaders can create more engaged teams, make better decisions, and cultivate a positive and inclusive work culture. Research indicates that mindfulness leaders are better equipped to manage their teams, handle stressful situations, and make strategic decisions that align with long-term goals (Boyatzis & McKee, 2005).

Mindful leadership's core is the ability to make better, more thoughtful decisions. In many workplaces, leaders must make rapid decisions under pressure, sometimes leading to mistakes, conflicts, or poorly considered choices. When leaders practice mindfulness, they develop the ability to pause, reflect, and evaluate different options before deciding. This practice allows leaders to be less reactive and more intentional. By cultivating the habit of pausing before responding to challenges or stressors, mindful leaders can make decisions that are aligned with immediate needs and consider the long-term impact on the organization and its employees. For instance, a study published in the Academy of Management Journal found that leaders who regularly practiced mindfulness could better process information, remain calm under pressure, and make more strategic decisions, even in complex or rapidly changing environments (Reb et al., 2014).

Beyond decision-making, mindful leadership is also deeply connected to emotional intelligence. Emotional intelligence (EI) is the ability to recognize, understand, and manage one's emotions while being sensitive to the emotions of others. Leaders with high emotional intelligence can better navigate interpersonal conflicts, inspire their teams, and foster stronger relationships within the workplace (Goleman, 1998). Mindfulness enhances emotional intelligence by increasing leaders' self-awareness—enabling them to become more attuned to their emotional states. When leaders are more aware of their emotions, they can better manage them, which helps them respond more effectively in challenging situations. In addition to self-awareness, mindfulness fosters empathy, allowing leaders to connect more deeply with the emotional experiences of their employees. This empathetic awareness helps leaders create a more compassionate, supportive, collaborative work environment.

Another essential component of mindful leadership is compassion. Compassionate leadership involves prioritizing the well-being of employees and creating a work culture that emphasizes empathy, care, and inclusivity. Studies have shown that employees who feel supported and cared for by their leaders are more likely to be engaged, productive, and loyal to the organization (Kegan et al., 2014). Mindful leaders cultivate compassion by practicing self-care and extending that care to others. When leaders model compassion, it creates a ripple effect throughout the organization, encouraging employees to treat each other respectfully and kindly.

Moreover, compassionate leaders understand the importance of psychological safety. This concept refers to creating an environment where employees feel comfortable sharing ideas, voicing concerns, and taking risks without fear of judgment or retribution. By fostering psychological safety, mindful leaders enable their teams to innovate, collaborate, and grow.

Innovation and creativity also flourish under mindful leadership. One of the defining traits of mindful leaders is their ability to remain fully present and open to new ideas. Mindful leaders approach each day with curiosity and openness, encouraging a culture of continuous learning and innovation within the organization. In today's rapidly evolving business landscape, where organizations must innovate constantly to remain competitive, having leaders open to new perspectives is vital. Mindfulness helps leaders stay flexible, adaptable, and open to feedback—essential for fostering team creativity and problem-solving. Leaders who practice mindfulness are more likely to create environments where employees feel empowered to explore new ideas, share their insights, and experiment with innovative approaches to their work.

In addition to these benefits, mindful leadership improves

work-life balance for both the leaders and their teams. Many leaders face immense pressure to meet organizational goals, manage teams, and navigate complex challenges, often leading to stress and burnout. Mindfulness provides leaders with tools to manage stress, avoid burnout, and maintain a healthier work-life balance. When leaders model healthy habits, such as taking mindful breaks, setting clear boundaries, and prioritizing self-care, they encourage their teams to do the same. This approach creates a more sustainable work environment where employees feel valued and are less likely to experience burnout. For example, leaders who regularly practice mindfulness are more likely to recognize when their employees feel overwhelmed and can proactively offer support or adjust workloads to prevent burnout.

Mindful leadership also strengthens communication and collaboration within teams. Mindful leaders are excellent listeners—they focus on being fully present in conversations, listening without judgment, and responding thoughtfully. This level of engagement fosters trust and transparency, encouraging employees to share their thoughts and ideas more openly. When employees feel heard and understood by their leaders, it leads to stronger relationships, increased morale, and a more cohesive team dynamic. Furthermore, mindful communication helps reduce misunderstandings and conflicts, as leaders are more aware of how their words and actions impact others. Leaders can resolve conflicts more effectively and create a positive, collaborative work environment by communicating mindfully.

Moreover, mindful leadership contributes to building a resilient organization. Resilience is adapting to change, recovering from setbacks, and progressing in adversity. In the business world, resilience is a critical factor in long-term success. Mindful leaders cultivate resilience in themselves and their teams by fostering a culture that embraces change and encourages learning from challenges. Mindfulness practices, such as reflection and mindful problem-solving, help leaders remain calm and focused in times of uncertainty. This approach helps leaders navigate challenges more effectively and models resilience for their teams. Employees who work under mindful leaders are more likely to feel confident in overcoming obstacles and adapting to change, ultimately strengthening the organization.

Numerous individuals, leaders, and organizations have successfully integrated mindfulness into the workplace, leading to remarkable improvements in employee well-being, productivity, leadership development, and overall workplace culture. These case studies highlight the transformative power of mindfulness and demonstrate its scalability across different industries.

One of the most well-known and pioneering examples of workplace mindfulness is Google, which introduced its mindfulness program, "Search Inside Yourself" (SIY). Developed by Google engineer Chade-Meng Tan, SIY was designed to help employees cultivate emotional intelligence through mindfulness practices. The program combines mindfulness meditation techniques with emotional intelligence skills training, such as self-awareness, empathy, and emotional regulation. SIY initially began as a small initiative within Google but quickly gained popularity among employees and became one of the company's flagship personal development programs. The results were striking: Employees who participated in the program reported reduced levels of stress, improved focus, and enhanced creativity. The positive outcomes of SIY were not limited to individual employees; it also had a ripple effect across teams and the organization. Google leaders credited the program with fostering a more mindful, compassionate, and collaborative work culture, where employees felt more engaged and motivated to contribute their best work (Gelles, 2015).

What made Google's SIY program particularly impactful was

its ability to equip employees with skills beyond mindfulness alone. By integrating emotional intelligence training, participants learned to communicate, manage interpersonal conflicts more efficiently, and lead teams with greater empathy. The success of SIY within Google also led to the program being offered to other organizations, making it one of the world's most recognized corporate mindfulness programs.

Another exemplary case of organizational mindfulness integration is Aetna, a health insurance company that introduced a comprehensive mindfulness program to reduce employee stress and promote overall well-being. This initiative was spearheaded by Aetna's former CEO, Mark Bertolini, who personally experienced the benefits of mindfulness and yoga after a life-threatening injury. Realizing how much these practices had transformed his own life, Bertolini made it a priority to offer similar resources to Aetna employees. The company implemented many mindfulness activities, including mindfulness meditation, breathing exercises, and yoga sessions.

The results were remarkable: Aetna reported that employees who participated in the program experienced significant reductions in stress levels, with stress decreasing by an average of 28%. In addition, participants reported experiencing improved sleep quality, lower levels of physical pain, and higher levels of job satisfaction (Wolever et al., 2012). The program also led to concrete improvements in productivity, with employees who practiced mindfulness becoming more focused and efficient in their work. This, in turn, translated to measurable financial gains for the company. For example, Aetna estimated that it saved approximately $2,000 per employee annually due to the increased productivity and reduced healthcare costs resulting from its mindfulness program.

Aetna's mindfulness initiative demonstrates the business case for integrating mindfulness practices into the corporate environment. By prioritizing employees' mental and physical well-being, Aetna not only improved job satisfaction and engagement but also benefited financially from increased efficiency and reduced health-related costs.

The healthcare industry, notorious for its high levels of stress and burnout among medical professionals, has also seen the positive impact of mindfulness. For example, Boston Medical Center (BMC) introduced a mindfulness-based stress reduction (MBSR) program specifically tailored to nurses and doctors, many of whom were experiencing burnout due to their work's emotional and physical demands. The program provided healthcare workers with tools to manage stress, including meditation, mindful breathing, and body scan practices. The program aimed to help healthcare professionals develop emotional resilience, which is essential in high-stakes, fast-paced environments like hospitals.

The outcomes of the MBSR program were profound. Nurses and doctors who participated in the program reported reduced stress and emotional exhaustion levels, improved focus, and enhanced job satisfaction (Horner et al., 2014). Notably, the program also positively impacted the quality of patient care. Healthcare workers who practiced mindfulness could better manage their emotional responses, remain present with their patients, and approach difficult situations with greater clarity and empathy. As a result, patients experienced improved care, and staff turnover rates at BMC decreased significantly.

In addition to formal mindfulness programs, many healthcare professionals have incorporated mindfulness into their personal routines to maintain mental health and manage the demands of their profession. For example, mindful breathing exercises and short meditation sessions between patient appointments have become standard practices for doctors and nurses seeking to recharge and stay focused throughout the day.

Beyond corporate environments and healthcare, mindfulness

has also entered the education sector. For example, the Mindful Schools Program offers mindfulness training to teachers and students to improve focus, reduce stress, and enhance emotional regulation. Schools implementing these programs have significantly improved students' behavior, concentration, and academic performance. Teachers who practice mindfulness report feeling less overwhelmed by the demands of their jobs and more connected to their students, fostering a more compassionate and supportive learning environment.

Mindfulness has proven to be especially beneficial in educational settings where students face high levels of anxiety and pressure. By introducing mindfulness into classrooms, schools create a supportive environment where students learn to manage their emotions, cope with academic stress, and build resilience. Teachers who incorporate mindfulness practices into their routines often become role models for students, demonstrating how mindfulness can be used for lifelong well-being.

These case studies illustrate the wide-ranging benefits of mindfulness across various industries. From tech giants like Google to health insurers like Aetna and hospitals like Boston Medical Center, the integration of mindfulness practices has led to measurable improvements in employee well-being, productivity, and organizational success. As more organizations recognize the value of mindfulness, these practices are becoming integral components of workplace wellness initiatives, leadership development programs, and employee training.

By fostering mindfulness in the workplace, organizations improve employee satisfaction, reduce stress, and create a culture that values compassion, collaboration, and innovation. As these case studies show, mindfulness can transform individual lives and entire organizations, leading to healthier, more productive, and more compassionate work environments.

Integrating mindfulness into the workday can be a transformative process that enhances productivity and improves overall well-being. Small, practical steps often make the most significant impact. Using simple mindfulness practices, employees can gradually cultivate a more mindful approach to their work and daily lives.

One highly effective practice is to take mindful breaks throughout the day. Many workers push through long stretches of work without pausing and resetting, leading to fatigue, reduced concentration, and even burnout. On the other hand, mindful breaks allow individuals to reconnect with their breath and body, releasing accumulated tension and stress. These breaks do not have to be lengthy—a few minutes of mindful breathing or a short body scan can restore energy and focus.

For example, during a mindful break, employees can pause to take a few deep breaths, consciously inhaling through the nose, filling their lungs, and then exhaling slowly. Another option is to take a brief body scan, starting by paying attention to the feet, moving up through the legs, torso, arms, and head, and noticing any areas of tightness or discomfort. This practice helps bring awareness back to the body, releases tension, and creates a sense of calm. Incorporating these short, mindful moments throughout the day helps prevent stress from building up. It ensures that employees maintain their energy levels, allowing them to remain focused and productive for longer.

Another crucial practice is mindful task prioritization. One of the most significant contributors to workplace stress is feeling overwhelmed by competing demands and a long list of tasks. Many employees begin their day by immediately diving into emails or tackling urgent tasks before assessing their workload. Employees can create a more balanced and efficient workday by introducing a mindful approach to task prioritization. At the start of each day, they can sit quietly and reflect on their tasks for five to ten minutes. During this time, they can ask themselves: "Which tasks are the most important? Which ones can wait? Where should I direct my energy today to have the greatest impact?"

This practice reduces the feeling of being overwhelmed and helps employees develop clarity and focus. Mindful task prioritization encourages individuals to approach their work intentionally, making deliberate choices about where to invest their time and energy. It also allows for flexibility, as employees can reassess their daily priorities, adjusting their focus as needed. Over time, this practice enhances productivity, reduces stress, and promotes a more thoughtful and organized approach to work.

Additionally, self-compassion is an essential component of mindful practice in the workplace. The modern work environment is often fast-paced and demanding, and employees can easily fall into the trap of being overly self-critical when things go differently than planned. Mistakes, missed deadlines, or a heavy workload can lead to feelings of frustration and inadequacy, contributing to stress and burnout. Self-compassion, however, offers an antidote to this cycle of self-criticism. It involves treating oneself with the same kindness, understanding, and care that one would offer to a close friend facing similar challenges.

Practicing self-compassion in the workplace means acknowledging that everyone makes mistakes, that setbacks are a natural part of professional life, and that it is okay to experience difficult emotions. When something goes wrong, employees can take a moment to pause and recognize their feelings without judgment. Instead of criticizing themselves, they can offer encouragement, reminding themselves that mistakes are opportunities for growth and learning. Over time, this practice fosters resilience and helps employees stay motivated and engaged, even in the face of challenges.

Self-compassion also encourages employees to set healthy boundaries, ensuring they do not overextend themselves or take on more work than they can handle. Employees need to recognize their limits and manage their mental and physical health, especially when faced with demanding workloads. By practicing self-compassion, employees can better prevent burnout and maintain a more sustainable approach to their work.

As readers reflect on how to integrate mindfulness into their workday, journaling can be a helpful tool for personal exploration and growth. Journaling allows individuals to track their progress, reflect on their experiences, and identify areas where mindfulness can make the most significant difference. Consider the following journaling prompt: "How often do you check in with your mind and body during the workday? What simple mindfulness practice could help you reduce stress at work?" By answering these questions, employees can gain greater insight into their current work habits and identify specific mindfulness practices that can help them reduce stress and improve their overall well-being.

In addition to journaling, employees can create a daily mindfulness plan that includes simple yet effective practices such as mindful breathing, mindful walking, or even short gratitude reflections. These activities can be integrated into existing routines, such as taking a mindful walk during lunch or practicing deep breathing before a meeting. The key is to start small and be consistent. Over time, these practices will become habitual, creating a more mindful and balanced approach to the workday.

Another exercise to help integrate mindfulness into the workday is mindful listening. In today's fast-paced work environment, communication can often become rushed or distracted, leading to misunderstandings and frustration.

However, Practicing mindful listening can transform how employees interact with colleagues. During conversations, employees can try to truly listen to the other person, giving them their full attention without interrupting or mentally preparing their response. This practice fosters deeper connections, enhances collaboration, and reduces communication-related stress.

Finally, to maintain a mindful work environment, creating opportunities for team mindfulness practices is essential. For example, teams can begin meetings with a few minutes of mindful breathing or a brief reflection on the meeting's goals. Incorporating mindfulness into team activities fosters a culture of mindfulness within the organization, enhancing collaboration and creating a more supportive work environment.

By integrating mindfulness into daily routines, employees can improve their well-being, enhance productivity, and create a more balanced and fulfilling work experience. Whether through mindful breaks, task prioritization, or self-compassion, these practices offer powerful tools for reducing stress and maintaining a positive, mindful approach to work. Readers are encouraged to reflect on their current work habits, experiment with different mindfulness practices, and make small, gradual changes to cultivate a more mindful workday.

References:

- Baer, R. A. (2003). *Mindfulness training as a clinical intervention: A conceptual and empirical review.* Clinical Psychology: Science and Practice, 10(2), 125–143.
- Caldwell, J., Smith, L., & LaVoie, N. (2001). *Impact of break timing on performance and well-being. Journal of Occupational Health Psychology*, 6(2), 145–150.

- Davidson, R. J., Kabat-Zinn, J., Schumacher, J., Rosenkranz, M., Muller, D., Santorelli, S. F., Urbanowski, F., Harrington, A., Bonus, K., & Sheridan, J. F. (2003). *Alterations in brain and immune function produced by mindfulness meditation.* Psychosomatic Medicine, 65(4), 564–570.
- Gelles, D. (2015). *Mindful Work: How Meditation Is Changing Business from the Inside Out.* Houghton Mifflin Harcourt.
- Goleman, D. (1998). *Working with Emotional Intelligence.* Bantam Books.
- Good, D. J., Lyddy, C. J., Glomb, T. M., Bono, J. E., Brown, K. W., Duffy, M. K., & Lazar, S. W. (2016). *Contemplating mindfulness at work: An integrative review.* Journal of Management, 42(1), 114–142.
- Horner, K., Rees, L., & Davidson, L. (2014). *Mindfulness in healthcare: Practical applications and success stories.* American Journal of Nursing, 114(6), 60–65.
- Hülsheger, U. R., Alberts, H. J., Feinholdt, A., & Lang, J. W. (2013). *Benefits of mindfulness at work: The role of mindfulness in emotion regulation, emotional exhaustion, and job satisfaction.* Journal of Applied Psychology, 98(2), 310–325.
- Kabat-Zinn, J. (1990). *Whole Catastrophe Living: Using the Wisdom of Your Body and Mind to Face Stress, Pain, and Illness.* Random House.
- Maslach, C., & Leiter, M. P. (2016). *Burnout: A Leading Cause of Poor Mental Health in the Workplace.* Cambridge University Press.
- Wolever, R. Q., Bobinet, K. J., McCabe, K., Mackenzie, E. R., Fekete, E., Kusnick, C. A., & Baime, M. (2012). *Effective and viable mind-body stress reduction in the workplace: A randomized controlled trial.* Journal of Occupational Health Psychology, 17(2), 246–258.

CHAPTER 13: MINDFULNESS AND RELATIONSHIPS

Mindfulness and Emotional Intelligence in Relationships

Emotional intelligence is a cornerstone of healthy and meaningful relationships. It refers to the ability to recognize, understand, and manage our emotions and those of others (Goleman, 1995). In relationships, this translates to emotional attunement, empathy, and non-reactivity. Emotional intelligence helps us navigate the complexities of human interaction, from building trust to resolving conflicts.

As a practice, mindfulness enhances emotional intelligence by cultivating self-awareness and empathy. By being present in the moment, we become more attuned to our emotions and the emotional states of others. Instead of reacting impulsively to anger, frustration, or jealousy, mindfulness allows us to pause, observe our emotions, and respond in a measured, thoughtful way (Siegel, 2007). This skill is essential in relationships where emotions run high, and reactivity can lead to misunderstandings and conflict.

Mindfulness also improves emotional regulation, a key component of emotional intelligence. By learning to observe emotions without becoming overwhelmed, individuals develop the capacity to manage their feelings effectively. This reduces the likelihood of overreaction, enabling more constructive communication during challenging moments. As we become more aware of our internal experiences, we are better equipped to express ourselves clearly and empathize with others.

In personal relationships, mindfulness fosters greater connection and intimacy. When fully present with a partner, friend, or family member, we can engage more deeply in the relationship. The other person feels this presence, creating a sense of mutual respect and understanding. Relationships built on this presence and emotional intelligence foundation are often more resilient and fulfilling.

Techniques for Mindful Relationships

Mindful relationships are those in which both individuals are fully present and engaged, free from distractions and judgments. Developing such relationships requires applying specific mindfulness techniques that promote effective communication and empathy.

One of the most essential practices in a mindful relationship is mindful listening. Mindful listening involves giving the other person your full attention without interrupting or formulating a response while they are speaking (Brown et al., 2007). This means being present not only in their words but also in their body language, tone of voice, and emotional state. Mindful listening helps build trust, showing the other person you value their thoughts and feelings.

In addition to mindful listening, mindful speaking is another technique that enhances relationships. This practice involves speaking with intention, clarity, and compassion. Before responding, take a moment to reflect on whether your words are necessary, proper, and kind (Kabat-Zinn, 2003). By cultivating mindfulness in your speech, you reduce the risk of saying something reactive or hurtful in the heat of the moment. Mindful speaking promotes clear and respectful communication, which is essential for maintaining healthy relationships.

Another crucial aspect of mindful relationships is mindful conflict resolution. All relationships face conflict occasionally, but mindfulness can help de-escalate arguments and foster a more constructive dialogue. One helpful technique is to pause during an argument and take a few deep breaths to center yourself. This moment of mindfulness can prevent you from reacting impulsively and give you the space to respond thoughtfully. Mindful conflict resolution also involves listening to the other person's perspective with empathy rather than trying to win the argument (Carson et al., 2004).

These mindfulness techniques are powerful tools for improving communication and reducing relationship misunderstandings. By practicing mindful listening, mindful speaking, and mindful conflict resolution, individuals can create more robust, compassionate connections with the people they care about.

Managing Relationship Stress with Mindfulness

Stress is inevitable in any relationship, whether with a romantic partner, a family member, or a close friend. Financial struggles, parenting challenges, work-related stress, and health concerns are just a few external factors that can pressure relationships. Additionally, internal stressors such as unresolved emotional wounds or insecurity can exacerbate tensions between people. When stress goes unchecked, it can lead to arguments, misunderstandings, and emotional distance.

Mindfulness offers a powerful antidote to relationship stress by helping individuals stay present, manage their emotions, and respond calmly and clearly. One way mindfulness manages stress is by promoting emotional regulation. When mindful of our emotions, we can observe them without becoming overwhelmed or controlled. This is especially helpful in relationships where intense emotions can sometimes cloud judgment and escalate conflict (Hülsheger et al., 2013).

Another benefit of mindfulness in managing relationship stress is that it fosters non-judgmental awareness. In stressful situations, it is expected to blame the other person or view the situation through a negative lens. Mindfulness encourages us to step back from these automatic judgments and see the situation more objectively. By adopting a non-judgmental attitude, we are less likely to react defensively and more likely to approach the situation with an open mind (Shapiro et al., 2006).

Practicing mindfulness during relationship stress also helps create a sense of emotional safety. When both partners commit to mindfulness, they create an environment where both people feel heard, understood, and supported. This emotional safety is essential for resolving conflicts and building trust.

Specific mindfulness practices can be particularly helpful in managing relationship stress. One such practice is mindful breathing. When tensions rise during an argument, taking a few deep breaths can help you calm your nervous system and regain your composure. Another technique is the "STOP" practice: Stop, Take a breath, Observe your thoughts and emotions, and Proceed with intention (Kabat-Zinn, 1990). This practice helps prevent reactive behavior and promotes more thoughtful responses.

Building Deeper Connections Through Mindfulness

Mindfulness allows us to cultivate more profound and more meaningful connections with others. At its core, mindfulness is about being fully present in the moment, and this presence is crucial for building intimacy and trust in relationships. When we are distracted or preoccupied, we may miss important cues from our partners, family members, or friends. Conversely, when we bring our full attention to the interaction, we create a space where the other person feels valued and understood.

One way mindfulness fosters deeper connections is by encouraging us to slow down and savor the moment. In today's fast-paced world, many people rush through their interactions without fully appreciating their time with loved ones. Mindfulness invites us to pause and engage with the present moment, whether sharing a meal, conversing, or simply sitting together in silence. This presence allows for more authentic and meaningful connections.

Another way mindfulness deepens relationships is by fostering empathy. Empathy is understanding and sharing another person's feelings, which is essential for building strong, compassionate relationships. Mindfulness helps us cultivate empathy by encouraging us to be present with the other person's emotions rather than being focused on our thoughts or concerns (Decety & Jackson, 2004). When we are fully present with someone, we can better understand their needs and respond with kindness and support.

Mindfulness also promotes vulnerability, which is critical to building deeper connections. Being vulnerable means being open and honest about our feelings, even when they feel uncomfortable. Mindfulness helps us become more aware of our emotions and gives us the courage to express them authentically. This openness fosters a sense of trust and intimacy in relationships, as both people feel safe sharing their true selves.

By practicing mindfulness, individuals can cultivate more profound, more fulfilling relationships. Through mindful presence, empathy, or vulnerability, mindfulness creates the conditions for meaningful connection and emotional closeness.

Case Study 1: Mindfulness in Marriage

Sarah and John had been married for ten years, but their relationship was strained due to financial stress and the demands of raising young children. They frequently argued, and both felt disconnected from one another. After attending a mindfulness-based relationship workshop, they began practicing mindful listening and conflict resolution techniques. Over time, they noticed a significant improvement in their communication. They were able to discuss complex topics without becoming defensive, and they felt more emotionally connected. Mindfulness helped them rebuild trust and intimacy in their marriage.

Case Study 2: Mindfulness in Parenting

Emily, a single mother of two, struggled with managing the stress of parenting and work. She often felt overwhelmed and reacted to her children's behavior with frustration. After incorporating mindfulness into her daily routine, Emily began practicing mindful breathing and pauses during challenging moments with her children. She noticed she could respond to their needs more patiently and understanding. Mindfulness helped her develop a more compassionate approach to parenting and improved her relationship with her children.

These stories demonstrate the transformative power of mindfulness in relationships. By applying mindfulness techniques, individuals can improve communication, resolve conflicts more effectively, and build stronger emotional connections.

Reflection and Personal Practice

Consider the following journaling prompt to integrate mindfulness into your relationships: "Reflect on a recent conflict or misunderstanding. How might mindfulness have changed the outcome?" Explore how mindfulness could have helped you stay present, manage your emotions, and respond with empathy.

In addition to journaling, practice mindful listening during your conversation with a loved one. Set the intention to be fully present and engaged, listening without judgment or interruption. After the conversation, reflect on how it felt to be fully present and how it impacted the interaction.

Mindfulness is a practice for individual well-being and a powerful tool for cultivating healthy, meaningful relationships. By bringing mindfulness into your relationships, you can foster deeper connections, improve communication, and create a sense of emotional safety and support.

References:

- Brown, K. W., Ryan, R. M., & Creswell, J. D. (2007). Mindfulness: Theoretical foundations and evidence for its salutary effects. *Psychological Inquiry*, 18(4), 211-237.
- Carson, J. W., Keefe, F. J., Lynch, T. R., Carson, K. M., Goli, V., & Fras, A. M. (2004). Loving-kindness meditation for chronic low back pain: Results from a pilot trial. *Journal of Holistic Nursing*, 22(3), 287–291.
- Decety, J., & Jackson, P. L. (2004). The functional architecture of human empathy. *Behavioral and Cognitive Neuroscience Reviews*, 3(2), 71–100.
- Goleman, D. (1995). *Emotional intelligence: Why it can matter more than IQ.* Bantam Books.
- Hülsheger, U. R., Alberts, H. J., Feinholdt, A., & Lang, J. W. (2013). Benefits of mindfulness at work: The role of mindfulness in emotion regulation, emotional

exhaustion, and job satisfaction. *Journal of Applied Psychology*, 98(2), 310-325.

- Kabat-Zinn, J. (1990). *Whole catastrophe living: Using the wisdom of your body and mind to face stress, pain, and illness*. Random House.
- Shapiro, S. L., Carlson, L. E., Astin, J. A., & Freedman, B. (2006). Mechanisms of mindfulness. *Journal of Clinical Psychology*, 62(3), 373–386.
- Siegel, D. J. (2007). *The mindful brain: Reflection and attunement in the cultivation of well-being*. W. W. Norton & Company.

CHAPTER 14: MINDFULNESS FOR PARENTS AND CAREGIVERS

The Challenges of Parenting and Caregiving

Parenting and caregiving are deeply rewarding, yet they come with significant challenges. Juggling the demands of raising children or caring for individuals with special needs can cause mental and physical exhaustion. Stress, time pressures, emotional strain, and the constant need for vigilance can easily overwhelm even the most devoted caregivers. The lack of personal time and the emotional rollercoaster of caregiving can lead to burnout and feelings of helplessness. Mindfulness, however, offers a powerful tool for managing these stresses.

Mindful caregiving involves being present, aware, and compassionate toward oneself and those in one's care. It allows caregivers to approach their responsibilities with more extraordinary patience and emotional regulation, which benefits the caregiver and those they care for. According to Siegel and Bryson (2018), mindfulness helps caregivers develop a "calm and connected" presence, which fosters better communication, understanding, and emotional support in family dynamics. For parents, mindfulness provides the space to respond to their children's needs without the added emotional reactivity that stress often induces. Studies have shown that mindful parenting improves the emotional climate in the home, reducing conflicts and increasing harmony (Duncan et al., 2009).

Furthermore, when caregivers practice mindfulness, they can acknowledge their feelings without becoming overwhelmed. This emotional resilience is vital in managing the day-to-day stressors of caregiving, especially when dealing with unpredictable situations or emotionally charged moments. Research shows that caregivers who incorporate mindfulness into their routine experience lower levels of stress, improved mental health, and greater satisfaction in their caregiving roles (Singh et al., 2010).

Mindfulness Techniques for Parenting

Mindfulness can be a transformative tool for parents. Parents can better tune into their children's emotional and developmental needs by staying present and engaged. This enhances the parent-child relationship and promotes healthier emotional regulation in children. Mindful parenting is not about perfection but about being fully present during interactions with children, whether during play, meals, or challenging moments. Here are some effective mindfulness techniques for parents:

1. Mindful Play: Being present during playtime can deepen the bond between parent and child. Mindful play involves engaging fully in the moment without distractions from phones or other stressors. For instance, parents can focus entirely on the activity and their child's emotional cues while playing with blocks or drawing. According to research by Duncan et al. (2009), mindful play strengthens the parent-child connection and creates a positive, nurturing environment.

2. Mindful Listening: Children, especially younger ones, often struggle to express their emotions clearly. Mindful listening involves giving children undivided attention and listening to their words, body language, and tone. By practicing mindful listening, parents can better understand their child's needs and respond in a supportive, empathetic way. A study by Medeiros and Sevier (2015) highlights that parents who practice mindful listening report stronger emotional bonds and fewer misunderstandings with their children.

3. Compassionate Discipline: Discipline is one of the more challenging aspects of parenting, often triggering frustration and emotional outbursts. Mindful parenting encourages compassionate discipline—approaching disciplinary moments with empathy, understanding, and clear communication. Instead of reacting impulsively to misbehavior, parents can pause, reflect on the child's perspective, and respond calmly. According to Siegel and Bryson (2018), this approach fosters long-term behavioral improvements and helps children understand the consequences of their actions without experiencing shame or guilt.

4. Self-Compassion: Parenting is demanding, and parents often put undue pressure on themselves to be perfect. Practicing self-compassion allows parents to recognize that mistakes are part of learning. Neff (2011) emphasizes the importance of treating oneself with the same kindness and understanding that one would offer to a friend. This is particularly important for parents, who often struggle with guilt and self-criticism. By practicing self-compassion, parents can build emotional resilience and model healthy emotional regulation for their children.

Managing Caregiver Stress

Caregiving, whether for children, aging parents, or individuals with special needs, often involves significant emotional and physical stress. Many caregivers experience burnout, a state of physical, emotional, and mental exhaustion caused by prolonged stress. Burnout affects the caregiver's well-being and their ability to provide adequate care. Mindfulness offers tools to help caregivers manage stress and maintain their well-being while providing high-quality care.

One of the most essential aspects of mindfulness for caregivers is staying grounded in the present moment. Caregivers often feel overwhelmed by the many demands on their time and energy, and mindfulness helps them stay focused on the task at hand rather than becoming lost in worries about the future or regrets about the past. By staying present, caregivers can approach each moment calmly and clearly, reducing the likelihood of feeling overwhelmed (Kabat-Zinn, 2013).

Mindful Breathing: One of the simplest and most effective mindfulness practices for caregivers is mindful breathing. When stress levels rise, taking a few deep breaths can help calm the nervous system and bring attention back to the present moment. Research has shown that mindful breathing can reduce cortisol, the stress hormone, and increase feelings of relaxation (Creswell, 2017). Caregivers can practice mindful breathing by taking a few minutes daily to focus on their breath, inhaling deeply and exhaling slowly. This practice can also be used in acute stress, such as when dealing with problematic behavior or an overwhelming caregiving task.

Body Scan Meditation: The body scan is another powerful mindfulness practice that can help caregivers manage stress. This practice involves bringing attention to different body parts, noticing any areas of tension or discomfort, and consciously relaxing those areas. Body scan meditation helps caregivers become more aware of the physical manifestations of stress. It allows them to release tension before it builds into more severe problems, such as headaches or muscle pain (Kabat-Zinn, 1990). By incorporating the body scan into their daily routine, caregivers can reduce physical stress and improve their overall well-being.

Self-Compassion and Stress: Practicing self-compassion is critical to managing caregiver stress. Caregivers often prioritize the needs of others at the expense of their well-being, leading to feelings of guilt or inadequacy when they cannot meet all demands. Neff (2011) suggests that self-compassion involves treating oneself with kindness, recognizing that it is impossible to be perfect, and acknowledging that caregiving is inherently challenging. Self-compassionate caregivers are more likely to take breaks when needed, seek support from others, and maintain their mental and emotional health, ultimately benefiting both the caregiver and the person in their care.

Fostering Mindfulness in Children

Children can benefit greatly from learning mindfulness practices at a young age. Teaching mindfulness to children helps them develop emotional intelligence, improve focus, and build resilience to stress. In a world where children are increasingly exposed to stressors such as academic pressure, social media, and peer competition, mindfulness offers them tools to navigate challenges with greater ease and emotional balance.

Mindful Breathing for Children: One of the simplest ways to introduce mindfulness is through mindful breathing. This practice helps children develop awareness of their breath and use it to calm themselves when anxious or upset. Semple et al. (2010) found that children who practiced mindful breathing improved attention and emotional regulation. Parents can teach their children mindful breathing by guiding them to take slow, deep breaths, focusing on the sensation of the air moving in and out of their bodies.

Mindful Body Scan for Children: Another beneficial mindfulness practice for children is the body scan. This exercise helps children become more aware of their physical sensations, which can help them better understand and manage their emotions. For example, a child who notices tension in their shoulders might realize they are feeling stressed or anxious and can use mindful breathing or another calming technique to relax. Research by Renshaw et al. (2017) indicates that children who practice body scans experience reduced stress and improved sleep quality.

Gratitude Practice for Children: Teaching children to practice gratitude can also profoundly impact their emotional well-being. Encouraging children to reflect on the things they are grateful for, even small things like a sunny day or a kind word from a friend, helps them focus on the positive aspects of their lives. Studies have shown that children who practice gratitude experience greater happiness and lower levels of stress and depression (Froh et al., 2011). Parents can foster gratitude in their children by encouraging them to keep a gratitude journal or by creating a daily family ritual of sharing things they are grateful for. Mindful Household: Creating a mindful household, where mindfulness is integrated into daily routines, can help children develop mindfulness skills naturally. For example, parents can model mindful behavior by being fully present during family meals, practicing mindful listening during conversations, and engaging in mindful activities such as yoga or meditation together as a family. By making mindfulness a regular part of family life, children learn the value of being present and emotionally aware, which can support their emotional and psychological development throughout childhood and beyond (Siegel & Bryson, 2018).

Case Studies and Personal Stories

Real-life examples of parents and caregivers who have introduced mindfulness into their homes provide robust evidence of the transformative potential of mindfulness. In one case study, a mother of two young children reported feeling constantly overwhelmed by the demands of parenting, often losing her temper and feeling guilty afterward. She noticed significant improvements in her emotional regulation after incorporating mindfulness practices such as mindful breathing and body scanning into her daily routine. She remained calm during stressful situations and felt more connected to her children, which improved the overall atmosphere in the home.

In another example, a caregiver for an elderly parent with dementia found that practicing mindfulness helped her manage the emotional strain of caregiving. By using mindful breathing and self-compassion techniques, she could cope with the stress of her caregiving duties without feeling overwhelmed. She also reported feeling more present and attentive during her interactions with her parent, which improved the quality of their relationship.

These case studies highlight the positive impact that mindfulness can have on both caregivers and those in their care. By practicing mindfulness, parents and caregivers can create more peaceful, supportive environments for themselves and their loved ones.

Reflection and Personal Practice

To begin incorporating mindfulness into their caregiving or parenting roles, readers can start by reflecting on the aspects of caregiving or parenting that cause them the most stress. A helpful journaling prompt might be: "What moments during caregiving or parenting feel most stressful for you? How might mindfulness help you manage these moments more effectively?" By identifying specific stressors, caregivers can apply mindfulness techniques to those situations, gradually building emotional resilience.

In addition to journaling, readers can practice mindfulness exercises with their children or loved ones. For example, they might try a simple mindful play activity, where both caregiver and child focus entirely on a shared activity, such as drawing or playing with toys, without distractions. Alternatively, they can practice a mindful breathing exercise, teaching children to use their breath to calm themselves when upset or anxious.

By integrating mindfulness into daily routines, caregivers and parents can create a calmer, more supportive environment for themselves and those in their care. Over time, these practices can lead to deeper emotional connections, greater resilience to stress, and a more fulfilling caregiving or parenting experience.

References

- Creswell, J. D. (2017). Mindfulness interventions. *Annual Review of Psychology, 68,* 491–516.
- Duncan, L. G., Coatsworth, J. D., & Greenberg, M. T. (2009). A model of mindful parenting: Implications for parent-child relationships and prevention research. *Clinical Child and Family Psychology Review, 12*(3), 255–270.
- Froh, J. J., Sefick, W. J., & Emmons, R. A. (2011). Counting blessings in early adolescents: An experimental study of gratitude and subjective well-being. *Journal of School Psychology, 46*(2), 213–233.
- Kabat-Zinn, J. (1990). *Whole Catastrophe Living: Using the Wisdom of Your Body and Mind to Face Stress, Pain, and Illness.* Delacorte Press.
- Kabat-Zinn, J. (2013). *Mindfulness for Beginners: Reclaiming the Present Moment—and Your Life.* Sounds True.
- Medeiros, C., & Sevier, M. (2015). The benefits of mindful listening in improving communication. *Journal of Communication Research, 47*(4), 489–506.
- Neff, K. (2011). *Self-Compassion: The Proven Power of Being*

Kind to Yourself. HarperCollins.

- Renshaw, T. L., Cook, C. R., & Bantum, E. O. (2017). The role of mindfulness in fostering emotion regulation in children. *Mindfulness, 8*(4), 1086–1094.
- Semple, R. J., Lee, J., & Miller, L. F. (2010). Mindfulness-based cognitive therapy for children. *Journal of Child Psychology and Psychiatry, 51*(2), 115–125.
- Siegel, D. J., & Bryson, T. P. (2018). *The Yes Brain: How to Cultivate Courage, Curiosity, and Resilience in Your Child.* Bantam Books.
- Singh, N. N., Lancioni, G. E., Winton, A. S., Fisher, B. C., Wahler, R. G., & McAleavey, K. M. (2010). Mindfulness training for parents and caregivers of individuals with developmental disabilities. *Journal of Child and Family Studies, 19*(2), 167–176.

CHAPTER 15: INTEGRATING MINDFULNESS INTO DAILY LIFE

The Importance of Consistency in Mindfulness

Mindfulness is a practice and a way of life that requires ongoing attention and dedication. The power of mindfulness comes from its integration into daily life, where it transitions from being an isolated act—such as meditating for 10 minutes in the morning—to a constant thread that weaves throughout all aspects of life. Whether during a morning commute, eating a meal, or engaging in a conversation, mindfulness brings the present moment to the forefront. This is why consistency is critical. By making mindfulness an ingrained habit, individuals can access its benefits throughout the day, not just during a scheduled meditation session.

Research shows that regular mindfulness improves emotional regulation, reduces stress, and fosters greater psychological resilience (Kabat-Zinn, 2013). This is because mindfulness helps rewire the brain to be more present-focused and less reactive, especially under stress. Practicing consistently can change how individuals respond to challenges, leading to a calmer and more thoughtful approach to life's difficulties (Brown & Ryan, 2003).

Consistency builds the "mindfulness muscle," where, much like physical exercise, the benefits compound over time with regular practice.

The importance of consistency cannot be overstated, as the brain responds to frequent mindfulness by creating new neural pathways that enhance attention and emotional regulation (Hölzel et al., 2011). Mindfulness practice encourages neuroplasticity—the brain's ability to reorganize itself by forming new neural connections. Over time, this neuroplasticity allows individuals to experience more profound calmness, even in the face of stress. Consistency also fosters patience and kindness towards oneself, which are integral to personal growth (Neff, 2003).

Incorporating mindfulness into daily life does not have to mean meditating for hours. Small moments, such as focusing on the sensation of your breath while waiting for the elevator, can cultivate mindfulness. Making mindfulness a consistent habit becomes less about setting aside time for mindfulness and more about living mindfully throughout the day.

Building a Sustainable Mindfulness Routine

Building a sustainable mindfulness routine can be challenging, especially when faced with the pressures of modern life. Many people struggle with setting aside time for mindfulness amidst their already-packed schedules. However, by adopting a flexible approach, individuals can create a mindfulness routine that fits seamlessly into their daily lives. This section provides a blueprint for creating a sustainable practice that does not feel like another chore but a natural part of daily living.

First, it is essential to set realistic goals. Many people give up mindfulness because they set overly ambitious daily goals—such as meditating for an hour—that are difficult to maintain. Instead, it is better to start small. Research suggests that even brief sessions of mindfulness practice, as short as 5 to 10 minutes, can yield significant benefits (Creswell, 2017). Gradually increasing the length and frequency of sessions as one becomes more comfortable with the practice is a sustainable approach.

Establishing a consistent time for mindfulness practice can help maintain the habit. For instance, individuals can practice mindfulness first thing in the morning, before bed, or during lunch breaks. By linking mindfulness to a specific part of the day, it becomes easier to remember and sustain the practice. Additionally, reminders—such as setting alarms or associating mindfulness with specific activities—can help reinforce the routine.

It is also helpful to incorporate variety into a mindfulness routine. Walking meditation, body scans, or mindful eating can break the monotony and keep individuals engaged. By diversifying the types of mindfulness exercises performed, practitioners can experience mindfulness in different forms and settings, making it easier to stick with the routine over the long term (Baer, 2003).

Lastly, it is essential to recognize that mindfulness is a journey, not a destination. Being flexible and forgiving with oneself is crucial in sustaining the practice. If a day goes by without formal mindfulness practice, guilt is unnecessary. Instead, one can mindfully acknowledge the lapse and return to the practice with fresh intentions the following day.

Mindful Habits for Everyday Activities

Mindfulness is not restricted to sitting still in meditation; it can be integrated into any activity throughout the day. This section introduces mindful habits for everyday tasks, helping individuals bring a sense of presence to even the most mundane activities. By practicing mindfulness in daily activities such as eating, walking, or even brushing teeth, individuals can stay connected to the present moment and cultivate a deeper awareness of their thoughts, emotions, and surroundings.

Mindful eating is one of the most accessible ways to incorporate mindfulness into daily life. Instead of rushing through meals or multitasking while eating, individuals can focus on the food's taste, texture, and smell, savoring each bite. Research shows that mindful eating enhances the meal's enjoyment, helps regulate overeating, and promotes better digestion (Kristeller & Wolever, 2011). Slowing down and paying attention to eating can foster a greater appreciation for food and its nourishment.

Walking is another activity that offers a perfect opportunity for mindfulness. Whether walking to the bus stop, during a lunch break, or around the neighborhood, individuals can practice mindful walking by focusing on the sensation of each step, the feeling of their feet touching the ground, or the rhythm of their breath. Individuals can transform a simple activity into a grounding mindfulness practice by being fully present during a walk.

Even routine tasks such as cleaning, brushing your teeth, or taking a shower can become opportunities for mindfulness. By focusing on the physical sensations of these activities— the feel of water on the skin, the sound of bristles on teeth, or the movement of a sponge across a surface— individuals can cultivate a sense of presence and peace during these otherwise mundane moments. Research suggests that integrating mindfulness into such activities can reduce stress and enhance well-being (Carson et al., 2006).

One of the core principles of mindfulness is that it can be practiced at any moment, regardless of the activity. Mindfulness is less about what you do and more about how you do it. By focusing on the present moment and fully engaging with whatever task is at hand, individuals can turn everyday activities into powerful mindfulness practices.

Overcoming Common Challenges

While the benefits of mindfulness are well-documented, many individuals face challenges when trying to maintain a regular mindfulness practice. Some common obstacles include lack of time, motivation, and distractions. This section addresses these challenges and provides practical strategies to overcome them.

One of the most frequently cited barriers to mindfulness is time. Many believe they lack time to dedicate to mindfulness, especially with work, family, and other responsibilities. However, mindfulness can be effective for long periods. As mentioned earlier, even short sessions can have a significant impact. Integrating mindfulness into existing activities, such as walking, eating, or commuting, can be helpful for those who struggle to find time. By practicing mindfulness during these moments, individuals can reap the benefits without needing additional time in their schedules (Kabat-Zinn, 2003).

Another challenge is maintaining motivation. Many individuals enthusiastically start mindfulness practices, but their motivation wanes over time. To overcome this, it can be helpful to remember the reasons for practicing mindfulness and to set small, achievable goals. Additionally, practicing self-compassion is crucial. Instead of criticizing oneself for missing a day of practice, it is essential to approach the lapse with kindness and understanding and then recommit to the practice (Neff, 2003).

Distractions are another common challenge. Whether it is the constant ping of notifications from a smartphone or the demands of a busy household, distractions can make it difficult to focus on mindfulness. One strategy for managing distractions is to create a dedicated mindfulness space free from interruptions. This could be a quiet room, a corner of the home, or even a spot in a nearby park. Individuals can reduce distractions and create an environment that supports focus by having a designated space for mindfulness practice.

Using technology mindfully can also help reduce distractions. While smartphones are often a source of distraction, they can also be used as tools for mindfulness practice. Many mindfulness apps offer guided meditations, reminders, and tools for tracking progress. By using these apps, individuals can incorporate mindfulness into their daily lives in a structured and supportive way (Lomas et al., 2017).

As you reach the end of this book, it is time to reflect on your mindfulness journey. Take a moment to consider how you can continue to incorporate mindfulness into your daily routines. Ask yourself: *What small changes can I make to bring more mindfulness into my life? How can I maintain consistency in my practice, even when life gets busy?* Jot down your thoughts in a journal to set clear intentions moving forward.

To help you establish a regular mindfulness routine, commit to one simple mindful habit for the coming week. It could be taking three deep breaths before starting your workday, practicing gratitude each evening, or engaging in mindful walking during breaks. Pick one practice that resonates with you and make it a daily priority. By doing so, you will experience how even small, consistent acts of mindfulness can create meaningful shifts in your well-being.

Remember, mindfulness is not just about formal meditation—it is about weaving moments of awareness into every part of your day. Whether through a few minutes of focused breathing, mindful listening during conversations, or simply appreciating the present moment, mindfulness is a tool that brings more peace, clarity, and compassion into your life.

As you move forward, approach your mindfulness practice with consistency, patience, and self-kindness. This journey is not about perfection but a genuine effort to be present and open to each moment. Embrace the growth, be gentle with yourself, and allow mindfulness to guide you as you navigate life's challenges and joys.

References:

- Baer, R. A. (2003). Mindfulness training as a clinical intervention: A conceptual and empirical review. *Clinical Psychology: Science and Practice*, 10(2), 125–143.
- Brown, K. W., & Ryan, R. M. (2003). The benefits of being present: Mindfulness and its role in psychological well-being. *Journal of Personality and Social Psychology*, 84(4), 822–848.
- Carson, J. W., Carson, K. M., Gil, K. M., & Baucom, D. H. (2006). Mindfulness-based relationship enhancement. *Behavior Therapy*, 37(4), 381–391.
- Creswell, J. D. (2017). Mindfulness interventions. *Annual Review of Psychology*, 68, 491-516.
- Hölzel, B. K., Carmody, J., Vangel, M., Congleton, C., Yerramsetti, S. M., Gard, T., & Lazar, S. W. (2011). Mindfulness practice leads to increases in regional brain gray matter density. *Psychiatry Research: Neuroimaging*, 191(1), 36-43.
- Kabat-Zinn, J. (2003). *Mindfulness-based interventions in context: Past, present, and future.* Clinical Psychology: Science and Practice, 10(2), 144-156.
- Kristeller, J. L., & Wolever, R. Q. (2011). Mindfulness-based eating awareness training for treating binge eating disorder: The conceptual foundation. *Eating Disorders*, 19(1), 49-61.
- Lomas, T., Medina, J. C., Ivtzan, I., Rupprecht, S., Eiroa-Orosa, F. J., & Hart, R. (2017). The impact of mindfulness on the well-being and performance of educators: A systematic review of the empirical literature. *Teaching and Teacher Education*, 61, 132-141.

- Neff, K. D. (2003). The development and validation of a scale to measure self-compassion. *Self and Identity*, 2(3), 223–250.

SERENITY & WELLNESS COLLECTION

Serenity & Wellness Collection is an empowering series thoughtfully crafted to help readers foster a more profound sense of inner peace, resilience, and holistic well-being, no matter where they are on their journey. This collection delves into the essential principles of mindfulness, emotional intelligence, self-healing, and balanced living, providing readers with practical tools to navigate the stresses and challenges of modern life.

The series features titles like Calm in Chaos, which offers strategies to maintain tranquility amidst the storms of life, and Cure in a Minute a Day, which introduces simple, daily practices for physical and mental rejuvenation. Each book in the series blends scientific insights with timeless wisdom, encouraging readers to build habits that promote mental clarity, emotional stability, and physical vitality. Whether learning to embrace stillness in times of uncertainty or discovering quick yet effective ways to support overall wellness, the Serenity & Wellness Collection is a comprehensive guide for those seeking relief, true transformation, and long-lasting peace.

This collection is ideal for readers looking to enhance their self-awareness, manage stress, improve relationships, or develop sustainable well-being practices. It is a reliable companion for anyone living a more mindful, healthy, and fulfilling life.

Cure In One Minute A Day

In today's fast-paced world, time is a luxury that most of us don't have. From the moment we wake up to the moment we go to bed, our days are filled with endless demands—emails that need answering, attending meetings, meals that need preparing, and families that need caring for. We are constantly being pulled in multiple directions, and self-care often becomes the first thing to fall by the wayside. We know we should care better for our bodies and minds, but when should we find the time?

For many of us, committing to long workouts, extensive meditation sessions, or complicated wellness routines can feel daunting, if possible. Yet, we all understand the importance of staying healthy, reducing stress, and maintaining mental and emotional well-being. The question is: How can we balance these needs with the realities of our busy lives?

What if you could start improving your health and well-being in just one minute a day? What if 60 seconds was all it took to start making meaningful changes in your life? It might sound too good to be accurate, but that's the idea behind Cure in One Minute a Day. This book is designed to show you that you don't need hours of free time or complex routines to feel better.

You need a minute—and the commitment to making that minute count.

The concept is simple but powerful. You can see real, lasting improvements by dedicating just one minute to your daily health. These brief but focused actions can help you reduce stress, boost your energy levels, strengthen your immune system, improve your mental clarity, and even enhance the quality of your sleep. Each chapter in this book provides a variety of one-minute practices that are easy to incorporate into your daily routine. They don't require special equipment, extensive preparation, or a considerable time commitment. They need consistency, and that's where the magic happens.

Why One Minute?

You may wonder, "How much can change in one minute?" The answer is a lot more than you think. Research shows that even short bursts of focused activity can significantly affect your body and mind. One minute of deep breathing can lower your heart rate and reduce stress. One minute of stretching can improve flexibility and circulation. One minute of mindfulness can enhance focus and help clear mental clutter. One minute of gratitude can rewire your brain to focus on the positive and boost your mood. These small actions can lead to significant results over time when practiced regularly.

The key lies in the power of habit. You create meaningful rituals supporting your well-being by incorporating these one-minute wellness practices into your daily life. These tiny moments of self-care may seem insignificant on their own, but their cumulative effect is profound. One minute may be a small investment, but when you repeat it consistently, it adds up to lasting change. This book teaches you how to make wellness a habit—not by overhauling your life, but by simply integrating short, manageable practices into your day.

Small Actions, Big Results

This book is not about quick fixes or overnight transformations. It's about building a sustainable approach to health and wellness, one minute at a time. You won't need to carve out considerable time in your day or disrupt your routine to see results. Instead, you'll discover that you can significantly impact your health in the time it takes to check your phone, make a cup of tea, or wait for your computer to boot up.

Each chapter focuses on a specific area of health and offers practical, actionable tips that take only 60 seconds to complete. You'll learn one-minute techniques for reducing stress, boosting your energy, improving your focus, enhancing your sleep, and even strengthening your immune system. These practices are grounded in evidence-based research and are designed to fit seamlessly into your life, no matter how busy you are.